Cambridge Elements

Elements in Defence Economics
edited by
Keith Hartley
University of York

THE POLITICAL ECONOMY OF AUGUSTINE WEAPONS

Keith Hartley
University of York

Shaftesbury Road, Cambridge CB2 8EA, United Kingdom

One Liberty Plaza, 20th Floor, New York, NY 10006, USA

477 Williamstown Road, Port Melbourne, VIC 3207, Australia

314–321, 3rd Floor, Plot 3, Splendor Forum, Jasola District Centre,
New Delhi – 110025, India

103 Penang Road, #05–06/07, Visioncrest Commercial, Singapore 238467

Cambridge University Press is part of Cambridge University Press & Assessment,
a department of the University of Cambridge.

We share the University's mission to contribute to society through the pursuit of education, learning and research at the highest international levels of excellence.

www.cambridge.org
Information on this title: www.cambridge.org/9781009627313

DOI: 10.1017/9781009627337

© Keith Hartley 2025

This publication is in copyright. Subject to statutory exception and to the provisions of relevant collective licensing agreements, no reproduction of any part may take place without the written permission of Cambridge University Press & Assessment.

When citing this work, please include a reference to the DOI 10.1017/9781009627337

First published 2025

A catalogue record for this publication is available from the British Library

ISBN 978-1-009-62731-3 Hardback
ISBN 978-1-009-62729-0 Paperback
ISSN 2632-332X (online)
ISSN 2632-3311 (print)

Cambridge University Press & Assessment has no responsibility for the persistence or accuracy of URLs for external or third-party internet websites referred to in this publication and does not guarantee that any content on such websites is, or will remain, accurate or appropriate.

For EU product safety concerns, contact us at Calle de José Abascal, 56, 1°, 28003 Madrid, Spain, or email eugpsr@cambridge.org

The Political Economy of Augustine Weapons

Elements in Defence Economics

DOI: 10.1017/9781009627337
First published online: October 2025

Keith Hartley
University of York
Author for correspondence: Keith Hartley, kh2@york.ac.uk

Abstract: This Element presents an economic analysis of Augustine's laws and weapons systems. It explores and evaluates their economic content and subjects them to critical analysis. The Element is both theoretical and empirical and the empirical work uses an original UK data set on military aircraft over the period 1934 to 1964. The period embraces major technical changes involving war and peace and the shift to jet-powered aircraft.

Keywords: Augustine, future, costs, economics, defence

© Keith Hartley 2025

ISBNs: 9781009627313 (HB), 9781009627290 (PB), 9781009627337 (OC)
ISSNs: 2632-332X (online), 2632-3311 (print)

Contents

1. Overview — 1
2. A Brief History of the Aircraft and Aerospace Industries — 5
3. *Augustine's Laws* — 9
4. Augustine Weapons: Alternative Approaches — 11
5. The Ministry of Defence Viewpoint — 12
6. Augustine Weapons Systems: What Are They? — 13
7. Causes — 17
8. Data Used in This Study — 19
9. Literature Review — 20
10. Evidence on Cost Escalation — 22
11. Cost Overruns on Civil Projects — 28
12. Unit Cost Curves — 29
13. Trainer Aircraft — 38
14. Empirical Results — 41
15. A Critique — 43
16. Future Challenges — 46
17. Overall Conclusions — 50

Statistical Appendices 52

Appendix I: Supplementary Data 52

Appendix II: Example of Contract Pricing for Canberra Jet
Bombers, 1953 61

References 63

1 Overview

1.1 What's in a Name?

Augustine weapons were originally named after Norman Augustine who was the then president and chief operating officer of Martin Marietta Corporation. The company merged with the Lockheed Corporation to form Lockheed Martin in 1995. His *Augustine's Laws* (Augustine, 1987) is a fascinating book written with a sense of humour and a tongue-in-cheek manner where the problems addressed are real and deserving of attention (Augustine, 1987, p. xiii). But the name has more illustrious connections.

The original Augustine brought Christianity to medieval England in the sixth century, starting in Kent and residing in Canterbury. Amongst his writings was the concept of the just war. This dealt with conditions under which the use of force is morally justified and how to conduct a war in an ethical manner. Augustine's ideas on the just war were widely discussed. However, this Element focuses on the Norman Augustine interpretation of Augustine weapons systems (AWS) and does not consider the ideas of St Augustine.

1.2 Introduction

Norman Augustine weapons are a new class of weapons systems. They are costly, high-technology systems with costs rising substantially between generations of equipment, reflected in intergenerational cost escalation. They offer the prospect of 'battlefield'-winning technologies and revolutionary warfare, which have great appeal to military staffs. Increasingly, capital and technology will replace military personnel. The emergence of remote warfare also raises ethical questions. Wars can be conducted remotely with operators in control centres located in different continents (Lee, 2019). Their high and rising real unit costs also raise the future prospect that wars might become unaffordable. Augustine weapons have further implications for a nation's armed forces and its defence industries.

Technology is an input into weapons with new technology resulting in new weapons. In turn, new weapons lead to substitution effects. History provides many examples. Guns, rifles and machine guns replaced swords, bows and arrows; castles were destroyed by cannons; radios replaced flags and pigeons; tanks replaced cavalry; helicopters are replacing tanks; steam power and then nuclear power replaced sail-powered warships; and nuclear weapons reduce the military advantage of large concentrations of conventional forces (Brauer and van Tuyll, 2008).

Augustine weapons involve revolutionary changes in military forces and defence industries. Alongside Augustine weapons, another new technology is emerging in the form of cheap drones, which can replace manned aircraft for attack and surveillance missions. Both Augustine and drone technologies will be assessed. Three questions are asked. First, what is known about Augustine weapons and drones; second, what is not known; and third, what do we need to know for sensible debates about these new weapons? The answers to these questions are: little is known; there is a lot which is unknown; and much needs to be known.

1.3 What Are Augustine Weapons Systems?

As already stated, Augustine weapons are a new class of costly, high-technology weapons systems that are experiencing substantial cost escalation between generations of equipment. Augustine concluded that the unit cost of high-performance fighters has grown by a factor of 4.0 every ten years, with cost growth closely correlated with the passage of time (Augustine, 1987, p. 140). 'New technology opens vast new capability vistas which are then crammed into each new generation of a product' (Augustine, 1987, p. 140). The capability vistas are represented by information technology, electronics, computers and computer software.

Augustine weapons offer the prospect of battlefield-winning technologies. The future will continue the trend of capital and technology replacing military and civilian personnel, with personnel becoming more skilled. The high and rising unit costs of Augustine weapons raise the future prospect that wars might become unaffordable. Augustine weapons and drones have led to the emergence of remote warfare, which raises ethical questions such as whether drones operated from Europe should be used to attack buildings and human targets in the Middle East or the Far East (Lee, 2019). These new weapons also have implications for the armed forces and the defence industries that need to be explained, evaluated and subjected to critical economic analysis, exploring the relationship between technology and weapons and their impacts on defence policy.

In one sense, Augustine weapons and drones are not new: like all weapons, they are lethal systems involving death and destruction, blood and ruins (Overy, 2023). Also, insofar as they require human inputs for their operation, such inputs form a constraint on the operation of weapons (and all weapons). Human beings cannot fight continuously without a break; they are subject to psychiatric and emotional stress as well as physical injury from gunshot and shrapnel wounds. Studies suggest that after sixty days in combat a serviceman is no longer militarily effective (Overy, 2023, p. 731). In future combat, artificial intelligence (e.g. robots) might remove the combat constraints of human inputs.

1.4 The Role of Economics

Economics stresses that a society's resources are scarce and have numerous alternative uses. There is the classic 'guns versus butter' choice which affects all economies. More resources allocated to defence means less for civil uses: more tanks mean fewer schools and hospitals. Military forces are not immune from this simple insight. They ignore it at their peril. Generals can have the latest tanks; admirals can have the latest aircraft carriers and their jets; and air marshals can enjoy state-of-the-art fighter jets and Augustine weapons; but none of these are costless. Something has to go: just as in any competitive economy, more expensive investments probably mean job losses. Certainly, high technology is not costless. Costly Augustine weapons come at a price. Being so costly, smaller quantities are bought with impacts on the size of armed forces and defence industries, forming the 'price' of Augustine weapons. The long-run impact of Augustine weapons is smaller armies, navies and air forces. For example, in the 1950s and 1960s, the UK Royal Air Force had some 1,000 Hunter jet fighters; by 2023, it had just 150 Eurofighter jets. Future trends are downwards.

Cheap drones have the opposite effects. They can be bought in large quantities and used liberally: they are not too costly to use and lose! Nor do they require specialised industrial facilities: small households and unskilled labour can be used for final assembly operations. But in their current form they are not as effective as Augustine weapons.

1.5 Military Forces

At a higher and rising real unit cost, Augustine systems will be bought in smaller quantities (fewer are bought at a higher price). In contrast, unmanned aerial vehicles (UAVs) can be operated by ground-based crews; they have substantial range and endurance; and they can fly for longer periods of time compared with manned surveillance aircraft such as manned maritime patrol aircraft. But today's drones are simple and limited in their military capabilities. For aircrews, simulators will replace actual operational flying, so reducing the wear and tear of operational flying with a reduced demand for replacement aircraft. Overall, Augustine systems need greater skills inputs for their operation, maintenance and repair, so there will be a greater demand for more highly skilled military personnel.

Drones will impact the numerical strength of the armed forces. Augustine weapons mean smaller forces, but this effect will be offset by opportunities to purchase larger quantities of cheap drones. There will be impacts on the training and support roles for military personnel. Simulators can be used for training, so reducing the need for costly manned training flights of expensive combat aircraft, with corresponding reductions in expenditure on maintenance and repair tasks.

However, cheap drones might be regarded not as substitutes for costly Augustine weapons but as complements. They might be operated jointly with Augustine weapons controlling 'swarms' of small drones both protecting the costly Augustine weapons and used as attack drones directed by the costly systems.

1.6 Defence Industries

Augustine weapons mean smaller volumes of costly systems for defence industries whilst drones mean the opposite, namely, larger quantities of cheap systems. Both types of weapon will mean defence industries becoming even more technology and research and development (R&D)-intensive. Augustine weapons will also create new demands for defensive systems, such as radar detection and defensive systems that are able to detect and destroy Augustine weapons (compare with the Israeli Iron Dome missile defence system).

Industry structure could be affected by a continuation of the long-run trend towards a smaller number of larger firms. National domestic weapons markets are likely to become smaller as nations find it difficult to fund costly Augustine systems, leading to incentives for international collaboration and a greater emergence of international firms. The twin technologies of Augustine systems and drones might be combined in one firm or lead to the emergence of separate specialist defence companies, much depending on the transaction costs of the alternative forms of firms.

1.7 Examples

There is considerable evidence in the UK and the USA of intergenerational cost escalation (Davies et al., 2011). Table 1 presents a few examples from a sample of UK fighter aircraft.[1] More examples are presented later in this Element. Two of the examples show cost escalation factors of 3.0 or more, namely, the Meteor and the Javelin. This sample is restricted to post-World War II UK military jet fighter aircraft. For the whole period 1946 to 1959, the aggregate cost escalation

---

[1] The UK data were from military aircraft contracts for the period 1934 to 1965. Unit costs are for airframes only, excluding other cost items such as engines, landing gear, radios and weapons.

Table 1 Examples of UK cost escalation

Aircraft	Date of first production contract	Unit production cost (£ – constant 1959 prices)	Escalation factor (real terms)	Time gap (months)
Meteor	3/1946	£45,591	x4.20	75
Hunter	9/1955	£47,143	x1.03	114
Javelin	1/1957	£147,051	x3.10	16
Lightning	4/1959	£189,168	x1.30	27

Notes:
(i) Escalation factor is the difference between the real unit production cost data for one generation of aircraft and its successor (e.g. Meteor to Hunter). The Meteor escalation factor and time gap were based on its predecessor, namely, the Spitfire (not shown in the table).
(ii) Time gap is the time in months between each generation of aircraft (e.g. time from Meteor to Hunter).
Source: DSTL (2010). All of the references in this Element are based on data extensively corrected by the author – corrections include data standardisation and adjusting current to constant prices using the UK Retail Price Index based on 1987 = 100. This resulted in a new and original data set created by the author.

factor was 4.20 in real terms, varying between 1.03 and 4.20 in real terms over a period of some thirteen years. The data provide evidence of UK cost escalation of varying magnitudes.

2 A Brief History of the Aircraft and Aerospace Industries

2.1 The Early Pioneers

Aircraft are the focus of *Augustine's Laws*, so a brief history of the industry is required. Aircraft represents a new industry showing the transition from a new entrant and an infant industry to an advanced technology industry. The first manned and powered flight in December 1903 was made by the Wright Brothers (USA). The early years of the industry were dominated by pioneering efforts reflected in different designs and materials used in the construction of aircraft. The early pioneers were mostly privately financed inventors relying on income from their main business activity (e.g. motor trade), the mail business, sponsorship from wealthy individuals, income from air shows, passenger rides, patents and prizes from competitions. The early pioneers built and tested their own new designs, where testing was not without considerable risks involving injuries and deaths for the pioneer pilots. There were also various 'races to be first' offering prize money (e.g. first to fly across the English Channel).

2.2 The Role of Government and Wars

Governments have been central to understanding the development of the aircraft industry through their demands for military and civil aircraft. For military aircraft, governments are major or monopsony buyers of military equipment and they can use their buying power to determine the size, structure, conduct, performance and ownership of aircraft and defence industries. With civil aircraft, governments have funded development and purchased aircraft for national airlines and their purchases have further affected industry size and structure.

Wars lead to a major increase in the demand for military aircraft and their quality is reflected in their technical performance characteristics. These characteristics comprise speed, range, altitude and weapons capabilities. Wars mean demands for aircraft that are faster and can fly farther and higher; there is an emphasis on volume production and new construction techniques emerging, as well as new materials, new designs and more powerful engines. These changes are reflected in the labour requirements for the aircraft industry in the form of numbers of personnel required and their skill levels. Wars also lead to new types of aircraft (e.g. bomber aircraft in World War I). Some new technologies are revolutionary, such as the jet engine and the rocket engines for the first generation of cruise and ballistic missiles (e.g. German V-1 and V-2 rockets built in 1941–42). Further revolutionary change occurred with the development of nuclear weapons (e.g. used against Japan in 1945) and the means of delivery (e.g. missiles and rockets).

2.3 The Inter-war Years

The ends of wars lead to opposite effects to the starts of wars, with disarmament resulting in reductions in demand, plant closures, mergers, exits from the industry, diversification and job losses. After World War I, the aircraft industry had to survive through efforts to develop civil aircraft. In the 1920s and early 1930s, the civil aircraft industry was an infant industry. Major developments occurred in the USA with competition between US airlines promoting innovation in civil aircraft. An example was the introduction of the Douglas DC-3 in 1936, which revolutionised air transport with its speed and range.

2.4 World War II

World War II provided further stimulus to the aircraft industry, affecting both the quantity and the quality of aircraft. Monoplanes replaced biplanes; aluminium replaced wood and fabric (the de Havilland Mosquito was an exception);

propellers became more efficient; undercarriages were retractable; and cockpits were enclosed. Imaginative designers innovated with advanced types, sometimes launched as private ventures. World War II also introduced the jet and rocket engines, which revolutionised both military and civil aircraft. Other revolutionary changes included the development and use of the first atomic bomb, the development of radar and electronic warfare (e.g. as in the strategic bombing of Germany in 1940–45) and the emergence of aircraft carriers and carrier-borne aircraft as new weapons of war. World War II also led to the emergence of mass production, enabling aircraft plants to achieve economies of scale and learning, and to replicate the mass production methods of the motor car industry. Here, the US aircraft industry had an impressive record. For example, it built over 15,000 Mustangs and 12,726 B-17 bombers and a total of almost 300,000 military aircraft in World War II.

By the end of World War II, the US aircraft industry was a world leader in civil aircraft, with an oligopoly industry dominated by Boeing, Convair, Douglas and Lockheed. The emergence of the Cold War led to an arms race in nuclear and conventional equipment between the USA and the USSR. Technical change was affecting the economics of the aircraft industry. Both military and civil aircraft were becoming technically more complex, costlier and taking longer to develop, leading to fewer being bought, making it more difficult to achieve volume production, especially in small domestic markets such as the European markets. Solutions to smaller volumes and rising unit costs included importing foreign aircraft and international collaboration.

2.5 Technical Progress

Technical progress led to major substitution effects with fighter and bomber aircraft replaced by missiles and rockets and atomic weapons replacing the traditional military advantage of large-scale conventional forces. Combat aircraft, missiles and rockets required greater electronics inputs, which led to the development of the defence electronics industry. Some aircraft firms acquired defence electronics businesses. Technical progress meant rising unit costs of military aircraft, resulting in industrial restructuring reflected in mergers, capacity reductions, diversification and exits from the industry.

Another example of technical progress concerns bombing by aircraft. Initially, during World War I, aerial bombing was undertaken by hand with pilots aiming by eyesight and dropping bombs from their aircraft. By World War II the technology had advanced and bombs were carried by aircraft and dropped by electrical methods initiated by aircrew (specialist bomb aimers). But this method was inaccurate and was improved to allow radar to guide accuracy.

Manned bomber aircraft were replaced by first-generation unmanned cruise missiles (V-1 rockets, March 1942) and first-generation unmanned ballistic rockets (V-2 rockets, December 1942). By 2024, bombing was automated and controlled by computers and electronics in extremely accurate missiles and rockets where pilots and specialist bomb aimers were no longer required.

After World War II, the jet engine revolutionised commercial air travel. The British de Havilland Comet jet airliner entered service in 1952 but suffered technical failures which almost bankrupted de Havilland. The US Boeing company developed a rival, the Boeing 707, which entered service in 1958. A new entrant to the civil aircraft industry emerged in 1970, namely, Airbus Industrie, which became a major rival for the US civil aircraft firms. Collaboration led to longer production runs, enabling European firms to compete with their US rivals. By the late 1990s, Airbus was a duopoly with Boeing in the world market for large civil jet airliners. Inevitably, controversy arose over the financing of Airbus aircraft. Boeing accused Airbus of receiving illegal subsidies in the form of launch aid, with Airbus responding that Boeing received subsidies from military and research contracts and state and local subsidies. In 2019, the World Trade Organization (WTO) ruled that the EU illegally provided support for Airbus and in 2020 the WTO declared that US benefits to Boeing violated trade rules. By 2021, the trade dispute between the EU and the USA over aircraft subsidies ended with a five-year accord to make sure that R&D support did not harm the other side with a move to a level-playing-field approach. Other nations became new entrants to the aerospace industry, including Brazil, China, Japan, India and South Korea. New entry meant more competition and innovation.

The next major technical change was the industry's move into space flight. In the meantime, the aircraft industry became known as the aerospace industry. The space race between the USSR and the USA started in October 1957 with the launch of satellites (e.g. Sputnik). The first crewed spaceflight was achieved by the USSR in 1961 and the USA landed a man on the moon in July 1969. The time-period from the first manned flight in 1903 to the moon landing in 1969 was less than seventy years, which is a further example of the industry's rate of technical progress. More recent developments have seen the privatisation of space involving the private finance and provision of both launchers and commercial space travel (e.g. Space X (Musk) and Virgin Galactica (Branson)). Privatisation meant that private finance replaced the industry's traditional reliance on state finance. One result was that wealthy individuals had a major role in the privatisation of space. Future developments include commercial space flights and greater militarisation of space. Overall, technical change has led to AWS (Augustine Weapons Systems), which are the focus of this Element.

3 Augustine's Laws

Augustine's Laws is a defining book that outlines fifty-two laws reflecting the author's experience at managing large aerospace projects. At times, the topics are treated in a tongue-in-cheek manner, but the problems addressed are real and merit in-depth analysis. This Element presents an economic analysis of *Augustine's Laws* which regards the tongue-in-cheek text as a set of serious propositions needing economic content, evaluation and critical assessment. Economics has a contribution to make to the debate and to the understanding of these new weapons systems. We need to know what is known, what is not known and what we need to know. Economists focus on costs in the form of opportunity costs and the sacrifices involved in selecting Augustine weapons.

3.1 Augustine's Chapter 16

The starting point is Augustine's chapter 16 dealing with the high cost of buying, which resulted in the most famous of *Augustine's Laws* (Law XVI: Augustine, 1987). Law XVI states: 'In the year 2054, the entire defense budget will purchase just one aircraft. This aircraft will have to be shared by the Air Force and Navy ... except for the leap year, when it will be made available to the Marines for the extra day' (Augustine, 1987, p. 143). This law was derived by projecting forwards in time the trend curves for the US national defence budget and the unit cost of tactical aircraft, which showed that in the not too distant future these curves intersect. This observation led to the formulation of what is known as the First Law of Impending Doom or the Final Law of Disarmament (Augustine, 1987, p. 143). Some commentators have suggested that the eventual outcome by the late twenty-first century will be one grand military vehicle – the Battlestar Galactica. An example of extrapolation at its best! Predictions have been made that the eventual outcome will be a single-tank army, a single-ship navy and Starship Enterprise for the air force! Applied to the UK, it was predicted that the UK will reach the single aircraft situation two years before the USA (Augustine, 1987, p. 144).

The high cost of buying chapter states that 'the unit cost of certain high-technology hardware is increasing at an exponential rate with time' (Augustine, 1987, p. 140). The point is illustrated with the example of fighter/tactical aircraft where the costs of each aircraft have grown by a factor of 4.0 every ten years, with unit costs closely correlated with time rather than with changes in speed, weight, maneuverability or other technical performance parameters. Similar trends apply to bomber aircraft. There is no ceiling or end in sight (Augustine, 1987, p. 141, fig. 19).

3.2 The High Cost of Buying Today

The same trend of rising unit costs applies to ships and tanks where their generally lower technology levels lead to lower unit cost growth by a factor of 2.0 every ten years. Rising unit costs over time of a similar magnitude are also apparent for commercial aircraft, helicopters, motor cars and houses, as well as 'certain other commercial products' (Augustine, 1987, p. 140). The cause of rising unit costs is that 'new technology opens vast new capability vistas which are then crammed into each new generation of a product' (Augustine, 1987, p. 140).

The electronic content of aircraft has been a source of rising unit costs, with the number of electronic component parts growing by a factor of 2.0 every ten years. Whilst the number of parts has increased, their capabilities have also increased enormously (Augustine, 1987, p. 125). There followed Augustine's Law XV: 'The last 10 per cent of performance generates one-third of the cost and two-thirds of the problems' (Augustine, 1987, p. 138). Next in the development of new technology is software, which was almost non-existent a few decades ago but has become the dominant element in the design of most major high-tech systems. The result is another of Augustine's Laws, Law XVII: 'Software is like entropy. It is difficult to grasp, weighs nothing, and obeys the Second Law of thermodynamics; i.e., it always increases' (Augustine, 1987, p. 152). Studies suggest that over the last twenty-five years, the hardware:software proportions of major systems costs have shifted from an initial eighty:twenty hardware:software ratio to a future ratio approaching twenty:eighty and that software grows by a factor of 10.0 every ten years. Augustine went further, suggesting that as the cost of various items within a family of products increases, reliability does not improve; instead, it worsens (Augustine, 1987, p. 158). He also had views on pressure groups: who were they and what were their specific objectives? His answer was 'no problem'; the group will find you and they will be vociferous about what they want, which is usually money. And there is valuable advice on the size of committees: the optimum committee has no members!

To summarise, the trends over time are for major weapons such as aircraft, warships and tanks to become more advanced technically; they are costly and becoming costlier. Rising costs mean smaller numbers with forecasts of a single-ship navy, a single-tank army and Starship Enterprise or Battlestar Galactica for the air force! The prediction goes even further with forecasts that by the twenty-second century there will be one single grand fighting machine encompassing a whole nation or perhaps a whole planet! There is, though, a contrary trend reflected in the development of small cheap drones, capable of undertaking some of the missions of costly Augustine weapons.

4 Augustine Weapons: Alternative Approaches

4.1 Lancaster's Approach

There are two further approaches to analysing Augustine weapons, namely, Lancaster's theory of demand and a real options approach. Each provides further insights into understanding Augustine weapons. Lancaster's novel contribution focused on goods being demanded not as goods but for their characteristics. For example, a cruise missile offers speed, range, lethality and accuracy in locating a target. Similarly, a fighter aircraft provides speed, duration, altitude and target identification. Some of these performance features might be possible substitutes, whilst others might be complements, with the whole package defined as a bundle of characteristics (Markowski et al., 2023). Different characteristics will be attractive to each of the armed forces and they will be combined into Augustine weapons offering their users 'good' value for money and ever more complex and costlier weapons.

4.2 Real Options Approach

A real options perspective can be used to analyse Augustine weapons. The design and development phase of a new weapon can be viewed as a sequence of real options. All weapons offer a range of design and development options. At the start, initial design work is required, followed by different stages of development leading to a technology demonstrator which, for aircraft, might offer prospects of flying before you buy. Each stage of development represents an option that might or might not be pursued, in such forms as modifications and product enhancements. For example, the Ministry of Defence (MoD) requires some new equipment that is not available off-the-shelf. As an alternative to offering a cost-plus or fixed price contract for development, the MoD could announce its willingness to buy call options from firms giving it the right to buy a specific number of units at a fixed price at some future date. There could then be a competition inviting bids and selecting the firm offering the best value for money option contract (Weston, 1996). This is not to imply that the use of real options methodology in the evaluation of procurement choices is simple and could easily be adopted. A major problem with defence investments is evaluating the gains: there are no measures of the value of defence outputs and usually it is assumed that inputs equal outputs, which is most unsatisfactory.

5 The Ministry of Defence Viewpoint

The UK MoD published a survey of evidence on the drivers of defence cost inflation (MoD, 2022). The survey dealt with defence cost inflation, cost growth and cost escalation. It defined intergenerational cost escalation (IGCE) as the change in cost between one platform and the next generation of a similar type of military equipment. In contrast, cost growth was defined as cost increases within a project. In reality, cost growth and cost escalation are often confused and combined into one concept.

5.1 The Main Drivers

The MoD survey identified the main drivers of IGCE as *economy-driven* factors and *customer-driven* factors. Economy-driven factors are those over which the government has little control, such as wage rates, equipment costs and other input costs. Customer-driven factors are ones where the government has more control, including equipment complexity reflected in performance characteristics arising from military threats, over-specification of proposals (gold plating), government regulatory requirements and declining production volumes.

5.2 Why Are Defence Goods More Expensive?

The reason why defence goods are more expensive than other goods is partly owing to monopoly and the associated monopoly inefficiency as well as small production numbers and export restrictions. Other factors contributing to IGCE include:

1. optimism bias, which is the tendency of appraisers to be optimistically biased about cost estimates;
2. poor understanding of risks and assumptions such as erroneous assumptions about the increased probability of cost growth;
3. changes in operational capability;
4. reduced competition in the UK defence market and the reduced number of suppliers;
5. use of non-competitive cost-based contracts;
6. procurement policy and incentives to develop new, less costly capabilities – often, the UK develops bespoke equipment rather than buying off-the-shelf from the world market;
7. moral hazard – human behaviour means that contractors have incentives to under-estimate costs and over-estimate benefits to win contracts;

8. workforce challenges – for instance, large projects may require the rapid build-up of the workforce, using inexperienced workers (who are less productive) and hence incurring higher cost.

5.3 Solutions

The survey proposed various solutions for cost escalation. These included improved procurement stability, with MoD publishing its long-term procurement plans and longer-term contracts. There were proposals for increased competition and more international cooperation. Also, it proposed addressing skill shortages, taking a new approach to industrial strategy, maintaining value for money in the absence of competition (e.g. via the Single Source Regulations Office (SSRO)) and increasing competition where appropriate. These proposals resemble a 'wish list' which is strong on 'buzz words' and demonstrates apparently great activity but lacks analysis and delivery. There remains a need for an economic model of cost escalation. Such a model would start from a trade-off between development time and development costs. For a given project quality (performance), a shorter development time is costlier: for example, you can land a man on the moon sooner, but at the expense of higher costs. This model predicts that cost escalation results from faster development (a time–cost trade-off) or from a choice of a more advanced project or from deliberate under-estimation of costs at the start of a project (Tisdell and Hartley, 2008, p. 384).

6 Augustine Weapons Systems: What Are They?

The basic distinguishing features of Augustine weapons appear to be clear. They are costly, high-technology weapons with rising unit costs over time. But how can AWS be identified? This section explores various different definitions, starting with the top 100 arms firms.

6.1 Identifying Firms Supplying Augustine Weapons

Table 2 presents potential suppliers of AWS. There is no published list of such firms, so Table 2 is a starting point. The list of potential suppliers was adapted from the SIPRI (Stockholm International Peace Research Institute) top 100 arms producers based on size of arms sales and shows the top twenty-five firms. Adapting the list from the SIPRI top 100 consisted of selecting those arms firms where 50 per cent or more of their sales were arms sales. This is an arbitrary cut-off point and reflects the view that AWS firms are large firms that are defence-intensive. Not all of the firms listed in Table 2 are potential suppliers; similarly,

Table 2 Potential suppliers of AWS, 2022 (the '(R)' against a company name indicates 'Russia')

Company	Arms sales (US $ millions)	Arms sales as share of total sales (%)
Lockheed Martin Company	59,390	90
Raytheon Technologies	39,570	59
Northrop Grumman Corp	32,300	88
General Dynamics Corp	28,320	72
BAE Systems	26,900	97
Rostec (R)	16,810	55
L3Harris Technologies	12,630	74
Leonardo	12,470	83
Thales	9,420	74
HII	8,750	82
Leidos	8,240	58
Amentum	6,560	75
Booz Allen Hamilton	5,900	64
Dassault Aviation	5,070	70
Elbit Systems	4,960	90
United Aircraft Corporation	4,820	72
Peraton	4,410	63
CACI International	4,679	72
Rheinmetall	4,550	67
Naval Group	4,530	99
MBDA	4,380	99
KBR	4,270	65
Israel Aerospace Industries	4,100	82
United Shipbuilding Corp. (R)	3,950	79
Sandia National Laboratories	3,920	89

Source: SIPRI (2024).

firms outside the list might be potential suppliers. To reiterate, Table 2 is only a starting point, presenting a list of firms on a subject where there are no published data.

Some potential suppliers of AWS might not yet exist. These are firms which are possible future suppliers. The space industry provides examples. In recent years, this industry has been characterised by new entrants in the form of private space companies. They include firms such as Space X (Elon Musk), Ispace, Blue Origin, Axiomatic Space and Virgin Galactic. Existing firms such as Boeing, Lockheed Martin and Nothrop Grumann are also involved in space. Foreign companies from China and India have entered the industry. The implication is that there is scope for new firms to enter the AWS industry and become new suppliers: we do not know who they are or which activities they might discover, but private markets will seek out potentially profitable opportunities.

6.2 An Alternative Method

An alternative method of identifying AWS firms comprises identifying firms that supply advanced technology and costly weapons: the weapons approach. Examples include combat aircraft, missiles, rockets, aircraft carriers, nuclear-powered submarines, anti-submarine frigates (complex warships) and tanks produced in the USA, Europe and the rest of the world. Representative projects include the US F-22 and F-35 combat aircraft, the Eurofighter Typhoon, the French Rafale, the UK ballistic missile and attack submarines, together with the UK Challenger 2 tank, the French Leclerc tank, the German Leopard tank and the US Abrams tank. The relevant data are shown in Table 3, which identifies Augustine weapons and their prime contractors, costs and quantities.

6.3 Augustine and Procurement Policy

Augustine weapons raise new issues for procurement policy involving the choice of contracts, supporting the defence industrial base and budget funding. For example, the US B-21 bomber involved a competition between two rivals, namely, Northrop Grumman and a joint team of Boeing and Lockheed Martin, with the former winning the competition. Questions arise as to how the USA will maintain its bomber industrial base to allow rivalry for any future bomber projects and the costs of such a policy (i.e. in terms of the sacrifice of other defence equipment?). Also, the current bomber project is being financed by a cost-plus incentive fee contract followed by a firm fixed price contract (CRS, 2021). Questions arise as to which type of contract will lead to the lowest acquisition price: a firm fixed price or a cost-plus contract? The literature suggests that cost-plus contracts promote cost increases and delays. But the

Table 3 Alternative methodology for identifying firms supplying Augustine weapons ('NA' indicates 'not available')

Augustine weapon	Prime contractor	Total programme cost (US $ billions)	Unit production cost (US $ millions)	Quantity
Combat aircraft F-22	Lockheed Martin; Boeing	60	143	195
F-35	Lockheed Martin	1.7 trillion development cost	131.3	2,470 (US orders)
B-2 Spirit Stealth bomber	Northrop Grumman	22.5	737	21
B-21 Raider	Northrop Grumman	203	700	NA
Virginia (nuclear attack submarine)	General Dynamics/ Electric Boat; Huntington Ingalls Industries/ Newport News	NA	4.7bn	2
US Ford-class aircraft carriers	Huntington Ingalls Industries/Newport News (one yard for US carriers)	12.998	37.3bn	10–11
Eurofighter Typhoon	Eurofighter	47.5 (UK only; 2011 prices)	124	558
French Rafale	Dassault Aviation	NA	115	259
UK astute attack submarine	BAE/Barrow, Cumbria	12.4 (2015 prices)	1.9bn (2015 prices)	7
US Abrams tank	General Dynamics Land Systems	NA	10.7	10,300
French Leclerc tank	Nexter	NA	17.4	862
German Leopard 2 tank	Krauss-Maffei	NA	31.6	3,600

Notes:
(i) Virginia submarines: acquisition costs are not available. Instead, only annual procurement costs data are available.
(ii) Data at early 2024.
Sources: CRS (2024); HC755 (2011).

alternative of a fixed price contract also has its flaws (e.g. it might involve firm bankruptcy and bail-outs).

The Virginia nuclear attack submarines raise similar questions about maintaining the US submarine industrial base. An annual procurement of two submarines supports two yards at the General Dynamics/Electric Boat Company and at Huntington/Newport News. Both companies have a shared industrial arrangement aimed at supporting both yards with alternate work on the reactor plants and final assembly. This two-shipyard strategy is costlier than a single-yard strategy, but it provides insurance against any yard failure. The strategy also retains key construction skills at both US shipyards (CRS, 2023). But the key issue is what are the extra costs of the two-yard strategy and will the resulting benefits make it worthwhile? Finally, questions also arise as to whether such costly projects should be funded by the service acquiring the project or by a special strategic forces fund where costs are distributed across all users and not restricted to a single service.

7 Causes

What are the underlying causes of AWS: why does the military always demand higher-technology equipment and why does higher-technology equipment lead to higher rather than lower unit prices? One answer lies in public choice explanations of the military–industrial–political complex (MIPC).

7.1 The Military–Industrial–Political Complex

The MIPC comprises interest groups of bureaucracies in the form of the armed forces and defence ministries, together with producer groups of defence contractors, each group pursuing its own objectives. The various groups include industrial scientists pursuing R&D activities, trade unions protecting the interests of their workers, together with local and regional associations representing local and regional interests. An international dimension emerges from international military alliances such as NATO (North Atlantic Treaty Organization). These various interest groups can be represented as agents in a principal agent framework. Agents are appointed by principals to achieve the aims of the principals. For example, in a profit-maximising firm, the owners are the principals and they appoint managers as their agents to pursue maximum profits. A problem arises since owners cannot be confident that managers might not pursue other objectives than maximum profits and might instead aim to maximise their own utility. Managerial utility comes in many forms, such as a 'quiet life' through on-the-job leisure or 'empire building' by hiring lots of attractive female secretaries or building brand new offices which give satisfaction to managers rather than the owners! On this basis, Augustine weapons are the result of agent behaviour in the procurement system.

Bureaucracies in the form of the armed forces and defence ministries act as budget-maximisers, which involves exaggerating the demand for their preferred weapons systems and under-estimating their costs. Defence contractors form producer groups which act as rent-seekers reinforcing the budget-maximising aims of the bureaucratic groups. Producer groups will also have strong preferences for profitable, cost-plus contracts rather than the incentive-based fixed price contracts. The language resulting from the behaviour of agents is predictable. A weapon must be purchased because it is 'vital for national security' and it will provide advanced technology for maintaining the technological competitiveness of the economy – and, of course, it provides 'lots of highly paid jobs essential for maintaining future living standards'. Inevitably, economists are critical of such arguments. They focus on costs in terms of the alternative use value of resources: would the resources used in developing the weapons system make a greater contribution to jobs, technology and exports if used elsewhere in the economy? Opponents of such questions often demand that the alternatives be specified and are critical when the alternatives are not identified. But economists respond by explaining that market economies will re-allocate resources to their next best uses reflected in market prices (e.g. such alternative industries as construction, aerospace, motor cars, engineering, pharmaceuticals and hospitality).

7.2 The Civilian Sector

Comparisons with the civilian sector are useful for assessing AWS and suggesting alternative explanations of these weapons systems. Technical progress in the civilian sector has resulted in many products that have become smaller, faster and newer, such as mobile phones, personal computers, TVs and motor cars. Homes are now examples of high-technology hubs: they provide food, entertainment and accommodation in air-conditioned environments. Significantly, the new-technology civilian products are often supplied at lower prices compared with Augustine weapons, which are costlier with each new technology and each new type. Specifically, Augustine forecast that rising unit costs of defence equipment would result in a single-aircraft future. Why does this happen? Why are the unit cost trends so radically different between civil products and defence equipment?

Standard economic analysis suggests various differences between price determination in defence and civilian industries. Possibilities include monopoly and oligopoly in defence industries and competition in civilian industries. These differences might be reinforced where defence markets are protected markets in which national firms are awarded national defence contracts. Or, defence equipment is a tournament good where the need to maintain military superiority requires equipment which is technically superior to that of potential rivals (Davies et al., 2011). Or, defence procurement contracts are cost-based with soft budget constraints compared with civilian contracts, which are fixed price with hard budget constraints.

8 Data Used in This Study

8.1 Overview

The data include some world-famous aircraft such as the Hurricane and Spitfire fighters, the Halifax and Lancaster bombers and the Mosquito from World War II. Post-1945 UK aircraft include the Meteor and the Vampire, the Hunter, Javelin and Lightning fighters, the Canberra and the V-bombers. The data available are from two distinct periods of war and peace. They also embrace major changes in technology with the introduction of the jet engine and the greater use of avionics. The data were extensively corrected by the author, so creating a unique and original data set. Corrections were made to ensure consistency and accurate costings, and data were converted to constant prices based on the UK Retail Price Index (based on 1987 = 100).

Actual contracts were available for the complete range of UK military aircraft comprising fighters and bombers of various types, trainers, transport and specialist aircraft, including air force and naval aircraft. During this period, aircraft firms emerged as specialists in fighters, bombers, trainers, and land and naval aircraft. Later, mergers in the UK aircraft industry reduced the number of firms and ended such product specialisation. The outcome by 2024 was a UK aerospace industry comprising a monopoly supplier of aircraft (BAE Systems), a monopoly supplier of aero-engines (Rolls-Royce), a monopoly supplier of missiles (MBDA) and a number of parts and components suppliers (e.g. Martin Baker ejector seats; PACE aerospace components; Marshall Aerospace aircraft maintenance, modifications and design). A number of UK aerospace suppliers were acquired by foreign firms. Examples included Dowty landing gear acquired by Safran (France) and Smiths Aerospace acquired by General Electric (USA).

8.2 Data Limitations

The data had its limitations. It reported only airframe costs and not aircraft costs, and reporting was not uniform: some contracts had missing data and not all contracts included the costs of jigs and tooling. Information was presented in current prices and was converted to constant prices with the details explained in the table notes. The information is also dated based on the period 1934 to 1964:

nonetheless, these are original data not previously published, and so they provide valuable insights into the pricing and cost side of the military sector of the UK aircraft industry. Interestingly, work on the original learning curve is historical, was first published in 1936 and was based on studies which first started in 1922 (Wright, 1936). The data allowed estimation of cost escalation for different types of aircraft and the shape of aircraft unit cost curves. In some cases, entry costs were estimated where there were alternative suppliers so that the unit costs of aircraft could be compared (e.g. where two or more firms produced the same aircraft).

9 Literature Review

9.1 Technical Change

Aircraft are a classic example of major technical change, starting with their very existence reflected in manned flight. But aircraft are not unique. Over time, most products have improved to become better, as shown, for example, by household goods and services. Consider the range of services now available within the household: communications (e.g. mobile phones), entertainment and leisure (films, TVs, sports), heating and eating (central heating, microwave ovens) and washing machines replacing laundries and the washing of clothes by hand. These changes have resulted in factor substitutions, with capital and technology replacing labour (e.g. a reduced demand for household servants).

Motor cars are a further example as they have progressed from early vehicles to today's complex machines, which are larger, faster and more efficient with engine technology shifting from petrol to electricity power. Airliners are another example of technical progress as they have developed to larger and faster aeroplanes, capable of flying greater distances. Space travel is the next 'new' frontier. Overall, in the civil sector, new technology usually leads to better and cheaper products. But defence is different: new technology is costlier. Explanations for this defence feature include defence as a tournament good, monopoly defence markets and aspects of procurement policies.

9.2 UK and US Studies

There is published evidence of intergenerational cost escalation for UK and US defence equipment. Real unit cost escalation of some 8.3 per cent annually was estimated for UK combat aircraft (Kirkpatrick and Pugh, 1983). A detailed study of UK defence equipment estimated real unit cost escalation at varying levels: 5.9 per cent for main battle tanks, 5.8 per cent for combat aircraft, 4.3 per cent for naval frigates and 3.8 per cent for aircraft carriers (Davies et al., 2011). A US study found annual real unit cost escalation rates of 6.2 per cent for surface combat ships, 5.3 per cent for attack submarines and

2.9 per cent for nuclear aircraft carriers with an overall annual cost escalation rate of 5.2 per cent for US naval equipment (Arena et al., 2006). Evidence from the USA shows that cost escalation on fighter jets was primarily caused (some two-thirds) by customer-driven factors in the form of equipment performance (vastly increased system complexity), enhanced features and higher quality, rather than by customer-driven factors (one-third) such as inflation and higher input prices (Arena et al., 2008). A further study by Johnstone (2020) re-examined the fundamental Augustine Laws to assess whether they are still applicable. It found that the Law forecasting that by 2054 the rising price of tactical military aircraft would exceed the US defence budget was 'clearly false' (Johnstone, 2020, p. 19). A similar conclusion was reached for civil airliners where cost escalation was estimated to be about half the cost growth in military fighter aircraft.

A Norwegian study examined cost escalation using controls for quality (e.g. speed, weight) and total production. On this basis, it found that the intergenerational cost escalation for helicopters, frigates, main battle tanks and fast patrol craft was close to zero (estimated at 1 per cent: Hove and Lillekvelland, 2017). A Swedish study based on Swedish defence equipment estimated cost escalation as varying: 7.6 per cent for infantry fighting vehicles, about 7 per cent for fighter jets, corvettes, helicopters and 0.7 per cent for battle tanks (Nordlund, 2017). International comparisons of cost escalation for similar types of equipment found that the Swedish figures were slightly higher than the international results, probably reflecting Sweden's traditional position as a small neutral country developing its own defence equipment (Amann, 2022; Hartley and Solomon, 2017). Whilst there is general support for intergenerational cost escalation, the different studies have their limitations. They use different definitions of cost escalation, different time periods and different samples of defence equipment; further, equipment differs between nations and some studies are in nominal and others in real terms. Also, estimating models differ between studies and there are confusions between defence inflation and cost escalation (Hartley, 2017). All of which leads to the perennial call for more data and more research!

9.3 Learning Curves

For the analysis of trends in aircraft unit costs, there is one common feature, namely, learning curves. These show a relationship between unit costs and quantity, with unit costs declining with increasing quantity. Labour is central to the learning curve which forecasts that unit labour costs decline with greater cumulative output. This reflects workers learning by experience or by 'doing': the more they repeat a task, the more efficient they become, particularly in assembly operations. The traditional learning curve was an 80 per cent curve predicting that direct labour input costs declined by 20 per cent for every doubling of cumulative output (Wright, 1936). Reality is different and actual learning curves differ from the 80 per cent curve. Increasingly, labour-intensive operations have become capital-intensive. For example, labour-intensive riveting has been automated with computer-controlled operations replacing manual labour. Critics also question the underlying theoretical basis of learning curves, arguing that 'the phenomenon is largely a creature of empiricism supported by a few theoretical constructs' (Baloff, 1966, p. 282).

10 Evidence on Cost Escalation

Little is known about the economics of AWS. This section addresses two questions. First, do these systems show rising unit costs in real terms between successive generations of such weapons, known as intergenerational cost escalation (the between effect: Markowski et al., 2023)? And second, do they show decreasing unit costs for a given type of weapon (the within effect)? These questions are addressed using an original data set from a sample of UK military aircraft.

10.1 Data and Sample

Data were obtained from actual UK procurement contracts for military aircraft purchased over the period 1934 to 1964. Military aircraft types varied amongst fighters, bombers, naval aircraft, trainers, transports and reconnaissance aircraft. Contracts showed the name and type of aircraft purchased, its weight, the name of the supplying firm, the dates of acquisition and delivery and the quantities purchased. Prices paid were based on unit production costs or average costs, which comprised labour and overheads, raw materials, bought-out parts and equipment, subcontracts, jigs and tools and flight testing. Unit prices consisted of average costs plus a profit margin.[2] Data availability varied between aircraft types with some contracts showing unit costs with and without the costs of jigs and tools, where jigs and tools costs might be some 10 per cent of unit prices. For some aircraft, unit cost data were available for alternative suppliers (i.e. where two to three firms manufactured the same type of aircraft), showing different overhead recovery rates between different plants. The sample for detailed analysis was selected to include pre-World War II, World War II and post-1945 aircraft. The task is to define and identify Augustine weapons. Augustine asserted that from

> the days of the Wright Brothers airplane to the era of modern high performance fighter aircraft, the cost of an individual airplane has unwaveringly grown by a factor of four every ten years. This rate of growth seems to be

---

[2] This study shows data based on unit airframe cost only, that is, excluding engines, landing gear, radio and guns.

an inherent characteristic of such systems, with unit costs most closely correlated with the passage of time rather than with changes in maneuverability, speed, weight or other technical parameters. (Augustine, 1987, p. 140)

For this study, a cost escalation factor of 4.0 every ten years is used as the strict definition of AWS, but other less strict definitions will also be used.

10.2 Case Studies

Table 4 shows trends in the levels and composition of unit cost data for UK fighter aircraft between the 1934 Gauntlet biplane and the 1959 Lightning jet combat aircraft. These examples allow assessment of *cost escalation* between generations of fighter aircraft and of any trends in the *composition of costs*. Augustine technical progress is expected to lead to changes in factor inputs between generations of aircraft. For example, higher-technology aircraft will require greater inputs of highly skilled labour. However, Augustine did not provide predictions on how the composition of unit costs was expected to vary between different types of aircraft. In the absence of such predictions, actual contract cost data are used to identify trends in cost composition for Augustine weapons (Sturmey, 1964). The research challenge is to identify AWS from the available contract cost data. Here, the research question is whether all combat aircraft are Augustine weapons?

Table 4 shows cost, price and profit data for UK fighter aircraft from 1934 to 1959. Between the Gauntlet and the Gladiator, real unit costs rose little, by a factor of 1.3 (gap of forty-one months); between the Gladiator and the Spitfire, real unit costs almost doubled (two-year gap) and between the Spitfire and the Meteor (seventy-five-month gap), real unit costs rose fourfold; between the Meteor and the Hunter, real unit costs rose very little (almost a ten-year gap); and from the Hunter to the Javelin involved a more than threefold rise in real unit costs (a sixteen-month gap), whilst the Javelin to the Lightning involved only a 1.26 rise for real unit costs (a twenty-seven-month gap). Overall, the data confirm intergenerational cost escalation but at varying rates. The data on shares suggest that after the Spitfire in 1939 came rising trends in shares for labour and overheads and falling shares for bought-out parts; the Javelin shares data appear to be an outlier.[3] Unit profit rates were higher for 1930s aircraft and lower for post-1945 aircraft.

Augustine forecast that costs would rise by a factor of 4.0 every ten years, but it was unclear whether the rise was in current or constant prices. The analysis in the previous paragraph assumed that costs would rise in constant prices. Table 4 is in both current and constant prices, allowing the hypothesis to be tested in both

---

[3] For the Javelin production contracts, labour and overhead costs were combined and presented as a joint cost.

Table 4 Costs, prices and profits for UK fighter aircraft

Variable	Gauntlet	Gladiator	Spitfire	Meteor	Hunter	Javelin	Lightning
Quantity	24	23	456	400	102	20	50
Date	6/1934	11/1937	12/1939	3/1946	9/1955	1/1957	4/1959
Unit production cost (£ current prices)	£,2027	£2,677	£5,470	£27,058	£42,160	£139,878	£189,168
Unit price (£ current prices)	£2,250	£3,050	£5,782	£27,750	£53,500	£150,368	£199,000
Unit price (£ constant 1959 prices)	£5,032	£6,468	£11,659	£46,757	£59,823	£158,079	£199,000
Unit profit	10.0%	10.0%	7.0%	3.0%	7.0%	7.5%	5.0%
Labour share	28.0%	22.0%	12.0%	12.0%	14.0%	87.0%	16.0%
Overhead share	38.0%	28.0%	14.0%	24.0%	33.0%	NA	46.0%
Bought-out parts share	29.0%	50.0%	64.0%	64.0%	47.0%	13.0%	35.0%

Notes:
(i) Current prices are at the date of the contract. For example, current prices for the Spitfire are at December 1939 related to the dates shown in the table. Quantities are numbers ordered at the contract date. Contracts are selected at the early stage where available.
(ii) Shares of production are where data were available. Shares are shares of unit production costs, for example the labour share of unit production costs. Figures do not always add to 100 per cent.
(iii) Constant unit prices are in 1959 prices based on the date of the Lightning contract.
(iv) Unit prices are based on unit production cost plus a profit margin.
(v) Only data for the Gauntlet, the Gladiator and the Spitfire include costs for jigs and tools. Bought-out parts share comprises bought-out parts and raw materials.

Source: DSTL (2010).

Table 5(a) Cost escalation for UK fighter aircraft ('NA' indicates 'not available')

Aircraft	Date	Unit price (£ current prices)	Cost escalation factor (current prices)	Unit price (£ – constant 1959 prices)	Escalation factor (constant 1959 prices)	Time gap (months)
Gauntlet	6/1934	2,250	NA	5,032	NA	NA
Gladiator	11/1937	3,050	x1.4	6,468	x1.3	41
Spitfire	12/1939	5,782	x1.9	11,659	x1.8	25
Meteor	3/1946	27,750	x4.8	46,757	x4.0	75
Hunter	9/1955	53,500	x1.9	59,823	x1.3	114
Javelin	1/1957	150,368	x2.8	158,079	x2.6	16
Lightning	4/1959	199,000	x1.3	199,000	x1.3	27

Notes:

(i) The data set did not provide data for fighter aircraft prior to the Gauntlet.
(ii) Escalation factor is the difference between the real unit production cost data for one generation of aircraft and its successor (e.g. Gladiator and Spitfire); n=7 fighter aircraft.
(iii) Time gap is the time in months between each generation of aircraft.

Source: DSTL (2010).

Table 5(b) Cost escalation for UK bomber aircraft (the minus sign '–' in the right-hand column indicates negative effects)

Aircraft	Unit prices (constant June 1959 prices)	Cost escalation factor (constant prices)
Hind	4,305	NA
Blenheim	43,542	x10.10
Battle	48,171	x1.10
Whitley	70,652	x1.50
Hampden	24,021	–
Wellington	28,947	x1.20
Stirling	69,172	x2.40
Halifax	70,310	x1.02
Mosquito	23,233	–
Lancaster	39,227	x1.70
Canberra	72,932	x1.90
Valiant	430,500	x5.90
Vulcan	348,500	–
Victor	246,000	–

Note: Aircraft are ranked by the date of the first production contract.
Source: DSTL (2010).

forms. Assume that the rise is in current prices. Ten-year periods are not available so approximations have to be used. Consider the Gladiator to the Meteor, which is almost ten years: the cost escalation factor in current prices was about 10.0 based on current prices in unit production costs or unit prices. For the next generation of fighters from the Meteor to the Hunter, giving a nine and a half-year gap, the cost escalation factor in current prices was under 2.0, well below Augustine's factor of 4.0. In total, the limited evidence gave some support for Augustine's strict hypothesis of costs rising by a factor of 4.0 in *current* prices.

Table 5(a) shows cost escalation for seven UK fighter aircraft. All the fighter aircraft in Table 5(a) showed varying degrees of cost escalation in current and constant prices. Between the Gauntlet and the Lightning combat aircraft over the period 1934 to 1959 real unit production costs rose by almost forty-fold. There were substantial variations in cost escalation between each successive generation and only the Meteor conformed to the strict Augustine prediction of unit costs rising by a factor of 4.0 every ten years.

Table 5(b) shows cost escalation for UK bomber aircraft. Most aircraft showed positive cost escalation, but there were some examples of unit cost reductions. The real cost escalation factor between the Canberra and the Mosquito, as light bombers, was over 3.0 and between the Lancaster and the Vulcan, both heavy bombers, it was almost 9.0. Comparing cost escalation for UK fighter and bomber aircraft (Tables 5(a) and 5(b)), the bomber aircraft showed some cost decreases and also showed some substantial real unit cost increases. Between the Hind and the Valiant, real unit costs increased by a factor of 100.0.

Overall, real cost escalation was observed for both fighter and bomber aircraft, with a median escalation factor of 1.3 for fighters and a higher median factor of 1.7 for bombers. The variation was much greater for bombers, with escalation factors of 5.9 and 10.1. Both propeller and jet aircraft displayed cost escalation and for fighters, cost escalation increased markedly with the shift from propeller to jet aircraft (i.e. Spitfire to Meteor: Hartley, 2023; Hartley and Sandler, 2001).

10.3 Case Study of Hawker Aircraft: 1938 to 1955

Data were obtained on Hawker fighter aircraft for the period 1938 to 1955. The data comprised all Hawker fighter aircraft over this period so that detailed study could be undertaken for a 'family' of aircraft, all produced by one company, embracing propeller and jet engines. For the complete period 1938 to 1955, the total real cost escalation factor was 6.1, varying between a negative value and a factor of 3.2. The results are shown in Table 6.

Table 6 The Hawker family

Aircraft	Unit price (1956 constant prices)	Cost escalation factor
Hurricane (9/1938)	9,073	NA
Typhoon (5/1943)	18,357	x2.02
Tempest (9/1944)	15,491	Negative
Sea Hawk (5/1953)	49,692	x3.20
Hunter (1/1955)	55,500	x1.07

Notes:
(i) The Hawker Hurricane, the Typhoon and the Tempest are World War II and propellor-powered aircraft; the Sea Hawk and the Hunter are post-World War II and jet-powered aircraft. Figures in brackets are for the date of the first production contract.
(ii) All cost data are in constant January 1956 prices. World War II prices are affected by price controls.
(iii) Cost escalation is for successive generations of aircraft. For example, from the Hurricane to the Typhoon is an escalation factor of 2.02, and from the Tempest to the Sea Hawk is an escalation factor of 3.20 (real terms).

Source: DSTL (2010).

The problem in comparing studies is that they are for different periods and embrace different types of aircraft and different firms. The Hawker case studies are for the same company and the majority of case studies show real cost escalation, with escalation factors varying between 1.07 and 3.20. Next, questions arise as to whether cost escalation is confined to defence projects.

11 Cost Overruns on Civil Projects

Cost overruns are not unique to defence projects. They also arise in civil projects embracing construction and private commercial projects. Cost escalation and delays often occur on construction projects, especially large construction projects such as airports, hospitals, bridges, railways, the Concorde supersonic airliner, the Olympic Games and software programs. Causes of cost escalation and delays on construction projects include reliance on initial estimate, site conditions, inaccurate cost estimates, project complexity and technical challenges, changes in project scope and design, inflation, regulatory challenges and selecting subcontractors on the basis of price. Ninety per cent of projects with a budget of over $1 billion go over budget or over deadline around the world; and the UK is not an outlier compared with the rest of the world (ICE, 2018).

11.1 Examples

A 1977 study estimated cost escalation and its determinants for a variety of sectors, including military aerospace, building and civil engineering and the private sector. Cost escalation was found in all these sectors (Hartley and Cubitt, 1976–77). Nor was it new; it occurred on nineteenth-century projects such as canals, railways, tunnels and bridges. Within the private sector, it was found in the chemicals, computer, electronics, engineering, pharmaceutical and textile industries. A study of cost escalation in the Norwegian road construction industry between 2009 and 2014 found cost escalation averaging 17 per cent. The main cause of escalation in road construction was change orders to the scope that were not covered by the original contract. There are other examples from the Olympic Games, the Panama Canal and the ITER (International Thermonuclear Experimental Reactor) project. The 2012 London Olympic Games were initially estimated to cost £2.4 billion, but the eventual cost was £8.8 billion. The Panama Canal extension had an initial cost estimate of $5.25 billion for completion by 2014, but its final cost was $6.1 billion in 2016. The ITER project to demonstrate nuclear fusion as a source of clean energy, which involved thirty-five countries, had an initial cost estimate of

€5 billion for completion in 2016, but the latest estimate was a cost of €20 billion to be completed by 2025.

A good example of the procurement problems for UK construction projects is HS2. The project was for a high-speed railway line running from London to Manchester and Leeds. In 2011, it was estimated to cost £32 billion; by 2013 its costs had risen to £55.7 billion; and by 2019 the estimated costs were almost £80 billion with completion expected by 2033. Against this background, the northern section from Birmingham to Manchester was cancelled in October 2023 after long delays and cost overruns as well as estimates that it would cost over £70 billion in 2019 prices, with some estimates suggesting costs as high as £170 billion. Also, following the pandemic, the business travel benefits of the project had changed and the project no longer provided 'good value for money'.

11.2 UK Government Advice

The UK government, through the Infrastructure and Projects Authority (IPA), published *Cost Estimating Guidance* in 2021 (IPA, 2021). It stressed the use of evidence-based cost estimates which are not a single figure but one that evolves over time as a range, depending on the level of risk and uncertainty. It also stressed that at the heart of a robust cost estimate are the three Ps, namely, principles of cost estimating, people involved in the estimate and performance reflected in the quality and consistency of cost estimates. The document outlined a best practice approach to cost estimating. One result of cost uncertainty for contractors was the inclusion of a price escalation clause in contracts. In the UK construction industry in 2021–22, the price indices for 'All Work' increased by 27.2 per cent to May 2022, with the largest increase of 64.9 per cent for concrete reinforcing bars (Weaver, 2022; Welde and Dahl, 2021).

Estimates of cost escalation for civil projects have some limitations. They might be based on current rather than constant prices and sometimes the price basis is not clear. Figures might be compared at different stages in project development (e.g. during initial design work and when nearing completion) and private sector projects might be shrouded in secrecy (e.g. private firms might be unwilling to reveal details of secret or cancelled projects).

12 Unit Cost Curves

12.1 The Predictions

Aircraft unit cost curves are expected to be downward sloping, showing falling average costs with increased output. Costs are of various types: short and long run; fixed and variable; average and marginal; and money and real (opportunity costs). The costs in this study are short and long run, fixed and variable, average and marginal and money expenditures. The contracts differ between aircraft and they comprise fixed (overheads) and variable costs (labour, materials, flight testing); some contain the costs of jigs and tools, different quantities ordered, and in some cases sufficient information is provided to enable estimation of marginal costs.

For some aircraft, there were second sources of supply so that unit cost data were available for alternative suppliers. These were World War II aircraft and those produced in the immediate post-1945 period. These data allowed an evaluation of the efficiency of procurement policy.

12.2 Learning Economies

Learning economies are a further source of decreasing cost for aircraft manufacture. Repetition leads to decreasing costs, with workers learning from experience and productivity rising with output. This effect is shown by data on unit prices, unit production costs and unit labour costs. Learning affects all these variables. Unit labour costs show the direct effects of learning, although these were not always available, hence the use of unit price and unit production cost data. The published data on prices, unit production costs and labour costs also have their limitations, which have to be borne in mind when interpreting the results. Published data are not necessarily least cost or X-efficient. They are simply observations and are not necessarily points on the same efficient average cost curve. Instead, they could be points on efficient cost curves, or points on inefficient curves or points on different curves reflecting different efficiency levels. These limitations apply to the empirical work reported in this study.

12.3 The Evidence

Evidence on unit cost curves is presented below for a variety of war and peacetime aircraft. The data are presented in two sections, namely, in the sections that follow and in the Statistical Appendices. The data presented here are for major wartime aircraft, namely, the Spitfire and the Lancaster, followed by post-1945 aircraft, the Meteor, the Hunter, the Lightning and two bombers, the Canberra and the Valiant. The data in the Statistical Appendices show supporting information for pre-war aircraft such as the Hind and the Hampden, for World War II aircraft, namely, the Hurricane, the Halifax and the Mosquito and for post-1945 aircraft such as the Vampire, the Venom and the Javelin and two V-bombers. The Spitfire is the first aircraft in the analysis.

12.4 Spitfire Fighter

The Spitfire was the classic World War II fighter aircraft which, with the Hurricane, fought in the Battle of Britain (details of the Hurricane appear in

Table 7 Supermarine Spitfire fighter

Date	Quantity	Unit price (£)	Unit production cost (£)	Unit labour costs (£)	Profit margin (%)
VS 12/1939	456	7,000	1,700	700	7.0
VS 9/1942	1,509	4,800	1,000	500	5.0
VS 8/1946	206	4,900	1,600	600	4.5
W 3/1941	50	6,900	3,600	1,500	5.0
W 6/1943	385	4,800	1,700	600	3.5

Notes:
(i) Prices and costs are in constant August 1946 prices (based on the date of the final contract for Vickers). Total output of Spitfires was 20,351. Spitfire performance varied widely even for aircraft with the same mark numbers. Over total output, there were 24 marks of Spitfire with different engines and different wings.
(ii) Vickers Supermarine (VS) was the original developer and was a subsidiary of Vickers Armstrong; Westland (W) was a second supplier. Costs in all tables are for airframes only. Prices in World War II were affected by price controls.
Source: DSTL (2010).

the Statistical Appendices). The Spitfire was a battle-winning aircraft with its contributions in the Battle of Britain and the rest of World War II (i.e. a successful aircraft). Cost-quantity data for the Spitfire are shown in Table 7. Spitfire unit prices and costs generally declined with greater output, although there was some evidence of 'tailing-off' towards the end of production. Westland, as the second supplier, was a costlier new entrant compared with Supermarine: for example, unit labour costs were £700 for Supermarine compared with £1,500 for Westland for early production contracts (in constant prices). The cost differentials indicate the price that the UK was willing to pay for a second source of supply. Profit margins for the original developer, namely, Supermarine, were also higher than Westland in early production.

12.5 Vickers Wellington Bomber

The Wellington bomber was included in the analysis because it achieved the largest output of all UK bombers: over 11,400 aircraft were produced in World War II. Cost details are shown in Table 8.

The Wellington was a decreasing cost aircraft, especially for unit production and unit labour costs: unit labour costs for the final output were some 60 per cent of those for the initial output. Profit rates also declined with output, falling from 7.5 per cent for the early output to 3.5 per cent for the final contracts (which was typical of wartime contracts).

Table 8 Wellington bomber

Date	Quantity	Unit price (£)	Unit production cost (£)	Unit labour cost (£)	Profit rate (%)
3/1940	133	16,928	6,015	2,560	7.5
6/1943	250	14,606	3,676	1,565	3.5

Notes:
(i) Data are in constant June 1943 prices.
(ii) The contract at June 1943 was the last contract with full details of prices and costs. The final contract was in December 1944, but this showed data only for unit prices.
Source: DSTL (2010).

Table 9 Lancaster bomber

Date	Quantity	Unit price (£)	Unit production cost (£)	Unit labour cost (£)	Profit margin (%)
AV 1/1944	3,570	23,600	4,300	2,600	3.5
AV 8/1945	931	17,700	5,000	1,700	3.5
AW 1/1944	40	38,900	16,800	5,700	2.0
AW 9/1944	next 200	18,700	4,500	2,000	2.5
AW 5/1945	329	18,500	5,100	2,200	3.0

Notes:
(i) Quantities, price and cost data are at the dates shown. For example, Avro (AV) was awarded a contract for 3,570 aircraft in January 1944 and received a final contact for 931 aircraft in August 1945. Armstrong Whitworth's (AW) quantity of 40 aircraft (first 40) was from a total order for 1,650 aircraft in January 1944.
(ii) While AV was the original developer for the Lancaster, AW was a second supplier.
(iii) Prices and unit costs are in constant August 1945 prices based on the date of the final contract for AV.
(iv) All costs include costs of jigs and tools. For example, jigs and tools costs might be some 10 per cent of aircraft unit costs. Some contracts did not make it clear whether costs of jigs and tools were included. If a contract did not make it clear, it was assumed that such costs were not included in the contract.
Source: DSTL (2010).

12.6 Avro Lancaster Bomber

The Lancaster bomber is included because it was one of the most famous aircraft of World War II. Its cost details are shown in Table 9.

Unit costs for the Lancaster declined continually with greater output, except for a 'tailing-off' effect approaching the end of Lancaster production (see unit production costs, Table 9). The costs of new entry were substantial, as shown by initial price and cost data for Avro and Armstrong Whitworth: for example, for early production, Armstrong's unit prices were some 65 per cent higher than Avro's. Profit rates for Armstrong Whitworth also varied, rising towards final output.

12.7 Gloster Meteor Jet Fighter

Data for the Meteor are presented because it was the UK's first jet fighter, followed by the Hunter and the Lightning. Meteor unit cost and price curves are shown in Table 10.

For the Meteor day fighter there were substantial reductions in prices and costs over total production: the 1952 prices and labour costs were 32 per cent of those in 1946 and unit production cost reductions were even greater. The night fighter version showed reductions for unit prices but increases for unit production and labour costs.

12.8 Hawker Hunter

The Hunter is included as a first-generation UK supersonic fighter. Its unit cost curves can be compared and contrasted with those of the Meteor (Table 11).

The unit price data show Hawker unit costs declining initially and then rising, followed by either a further rise or a fall, depending on the relevant cost curve. Overall, between 1955 and 1957, unit price and production costs declined to

Table 10 Meteor cost curves

Date	Quantity	Unit price (£)	Unit production cost (£)	Unit labour cost (£)	Profit rate (%)
3/1946	400	39,128	38,148	4,526	3.0
5/1952	150	12,697	9,358	1,470	5.8
11/1951 (NF)	200	28,728	11,937	3,132	5.4
8/1953 (NF)	200	20,250	14,415	3,727	3.5

Notes:
(i) NF is the night fighter version requiring greater factor inputs, as reflected in the unit price data.
(ii) The contract for May 1952 was chosen because it provides detailed cost data. The next contract for December 1953 provides data on unit prices only.
(iii) Data are in constant May 1952 prices.
Source: DSTL (2010).

Table 11 Hunter unit costs

Date	Quantity	Unit price (£)	Unit production cost (£)	Unit labour cost (£)	Profitability (%)
1/1955	200	54,200	47,700	7,600	7.0
9/1955	102	40,600	38,000	5,400	7.0
7/1956	217	44,400	41,400	5,800	7.0
11/1957	66	46,700	40,100	5,400	6.0

Notes:
(i) Data are for all contracts awarded to Hawker, Kingston; other contracts, which are not shown, were awarded to Hawker Blackpool (211 aircraft) and Armstrong Whitworth (249 aircraft). The data do not include the costs of jigs and tools.
(ii) All data are in constant 1957 prices based on the final contract for Hawker (November 1957).
Source: DSTL (2010).

some 85–84 per cent and labour costs fell to 71 per cent of their initial levels. Compared with the Meteor, the reductions in prices and costs for the Hunter were much less. This probably reflected smaller cumulative output and less learning for the Hunter.

12.9 English Electric Lightning

The Lightning is included as a third-generation fighter capable of much greater speeds than the Meteor and the Hunter. The unit price and cost curves for the Lightning declined initially, then generally rose, with some higher costs reflecting a shift to trainer aircraft and the reorganisation of the UK aircraft industry (Table 12). Certainly, after the second contract there is no evidence of decreasing costs. Profitability varied between contracts. Interestingly, it reached its highest level for the final contract: this is surprising since it was expected that profit rates would decline towards the end of production.

12.10 Jet Bombers

This section focuses on jet bombers and covers the Canberra and the Valiant. The Statistical Appendices cover the other V-bombers, namely, the Victor and the Vulcan.

12.10.1 English Electric Canberra Bomber

A total of 900 Canberra aircraft were built in the UK, with the first order for 132 aircraft comprising 90 Mark 1 bomber versions, 34 photo reconnaissance (PR)

Table 12 Unit costs for the Lightning

Date	Quantity	Unit price (£)	Unit production cost (£)	Unit labour costs (£)	Profitability (%)
4/1959	50	223,200	212,300	36,200	5.0
11/1959	47	178,100	165,000	25,800	5.0
11/1959	42	186,700	175,900	28,700	5.0
12/1960	19	255,600	232,600	40,100	4.5
12/1961	45	231,000	216,900	33,900	4.5
7/1962	20	329,800	308,600	52,300	7.0
1/1964	33	275,500	245,800	38,700	7.5

Notes:
(i) All prices and costs are in constant January 1964 prices.
(ii) Costs do not include jigs and tools.
(iii) Total UK output for the Lightning was 276 units, including development aircraft. Orders were for small batches of some twenty to fifty aircraft.
(iv) The July 1962 contract was shared between English Electric and Bristol as part of the newly merged firm of BAC.
(v) Data excluded details of a contract for twenty development aircraft.
(vi) Contracts for December 1960 and July 1962 were for trainer aircraft. All other contracts were for Marks 1, 2 and 3 aircraft.
Source: DSTL (2010).

versions and 8 trainers. Interestingly, even with a total UK output of 900 aircraft, UK orders for the Canberra were usually in relatively small quantities (e.g. batches of 25–35 aircraft). The final contract was in 1958.

Table 13 shows the Canberra as a decreasing cost aircraft with the 1953 aircraft some 90 per cent of the prices and production costs of the 1951 aircraft. The reductions in unit labour costs were more dramatic, at 74 per cent of these costs for the 1951 aircraft.

English Electric was the original developer for the Canberra, showing decreasing costs. Between 1951 and 1953 there were small reductions in prices and costs but substantial reductions in unit labour costs. Avro, Handley Page and Short Bros were alternative suppliers of the aircraft. Generally, English Electric as the original developer was the least cost supplier, apart from the unit labour costs for Avro. Each new entrant was a higher cost supplier. Because of Short Bros' position receiving state support in Northern Ireland, it was expected to be the highest cost supplier: in fact, it was not the highest cost supplier in the group. This distinction fell to Avro on unit prices and production costs. However, Short Bros received favourable treatment, reflected in its receipt of the highest profit rate of the firms (Table 14). Each alternative supplier was a decreasing cost firm. For example,

Table 13 Unit costs for Canberra

Date	Quantity	Unit price (£)	Unit production cost (£)	Unit labour cost (£)	Profit margin (%)
June 1951	90	60,480	57,184	15,288	6.0
Feb 1953	167	55,000	52,492	11,368	5.0

Notes:
(i) All data are in constant February 1953 prices.
(ii) The February 1953 contract was chosen because it was the last one to show unit production cost and unit labour cost data. All other contracts show unit price data only; the final contract was September 1958.
(iii) Data were available for the Canberra showing unit costs for different production plants; these are shown in Table 14.
Source: DSTL (2010).

Avro's unit labour costs at batch 21–75 units were 67 per cent of their level at batch 1–20 units and in July 1953 Short Bros' unit price at batch 21–23 units was 75 per cent of its level for batch 1–2 units. Short Bros also received a contribution of £90,000 per aircraft for the costs of jigs and tools for its PR9 aircraft.

12.10.2 Vickers Valiant Bomber

The Valiant Bomber was the first of the three V-bombers. Two prototypes cost £2.78 million (combined cost at 1955 prices). Unit price data show the Valiant as a decreasing cost aircraft, with unit price falling some 35 per cent over the production run from 25 to 190 units – the unit price of £385,000 for the first 25 units fell to £250,000 for the final contract (Table 15).

12.11 The Efficiency of Procurement

Overall, the evidence presented shows aircraft as a decreasing cost industry. Cost reductions were especially substantial for unit labour costs, which are more accurate reflections of learning curves.

The evidence on second suppliers allows an assessment of the efficiency of alternative suppliers. Typically, alternative suppliers were higher unit cost firms and the additional costs were substantial. For example, on the Spitfire and the Lancaster, unit labour costs for the second supplier were about double the costs for the original developer. But this was the price the UK was willing to pay for a second supplier in wartime, where the emphasis was on availability and supply rather than a narrow interpretation of efficiency.

Table 14 The Canberra and alternative suppliers

Firm	Time	Output	Unit price (£)	Unit production cost (£)	Unit labour cost (£)	Profit rate (%)
English Electric	6/1951	90	57,200	54,200	14,500	6.0
	2/1953	109	55,600	53,000	10,700	5.0
Avro	10/1953	75	81,800	76,800	8,900	6.5
Handley Page	8/1953	75	69,100	65,400	19,000	6.0
Short Bros	7/1953	60	74,100	68,600	17,000	8.0

Notes:
(i) All price and cost data in constant January 1955 prices (based on the date of the last contract, which was Avro's).
(ii) Firms selected to give similar quantities of contracts: Avro and Handley Page contracts were identical, with Short Bros slightly smaller. Contracts for prototypes were excluded.
(iii) The English Electric contracts for 1951 and 1953 contracts were for the BMk2 version: hence for the same aircraft.

Source: DSTL (2010).

Table 15 Valiant unit costs

Date	Quantity	Unit price (£)
9/1955	25	385,000
9/1955	24	338,000
9/1955	17	305,500
9/1955	62	260,000
9/1955	62	250,000

Notes
 (i) All contracts are at September 1955 constant prices.
 (ii) No data are available on unit production and labour costs and profits for the September 1955 contracts.
 (iii) Total production for the Valiant was 190 units over five production contracts.
Source: DSTL (2010).

A similar problem occurred with the efficiency of the procurement of the UK's three V-bombers. Efficiency, interpreted narrowly, required the procurement of one type of V-bomber rather than three types. A total of 435 V-bombers were purchased in their three variants. If 435 units of one type had been purchased there would have been savings of two R&D bills and the economies of scale and learning from a longer production run. To illustrate the possibilities, assume that only the Victor had been purchased. The savings that would have been achieved through not needing two extra R&D bills would have totalled some £10 million and unit production costs would have been reduced by 20 per cent or some £23.3 million (at 1955–56 prices). The total savings in R&D and productions costs by purchasing just one type of V-bomber might therefore have been around £33 million, which was a substantial number of sacrificed schools, hospitals and roads (at 1955–56 prices). This was the price paid for an insurance policy provided by selecting three V-bombers. Economic efficiency requires that these extra costs be viewed as representing a worthwhile investment.

13 Trainer Aircraft

13.1 The Sample

Unit price and cost escalation data for non-combat aircraft, namely, trainer aircraft are shown in Tables 16 and 17. Unit prices have risen from some £1,400 for the 1939 Tiger Moth to £233,400 for the supersonic Lightning in 1960, a rise by a factor of 168.0 in real terms over the whole period.

The Political Economy of Augustine Weapons

Table 16 Trainer aircraft

Aircraft	Date of contract	Unit price (£ – constant 1960 prices)
Airspeed Oxford	May 1938	9,770
Miles Magister	June 1938	4,215
Tiger Moth	January 1939	1,392
Miles Master	September 1940	15,542
Boulton Paul Balliol	February 1947	34,164
Gloster Meteor	August 1947	21,310
de Havilland Chipmunk	February 1949	3,273
Vickers Varsity	January 1952	67,878
English Electric Canberra	February 1953	75,248
Percival Provost	February 1953	20,945
de Havilland Vampire	May 1953	27,422
Hunting Jet Provost	July 1957	17,276
Hawker Hunter	October 1958	71,018
English Electric Lightning	December 1960	233,400

Notes:
(i) Date of contract is the date of the first contract or the earliest contract if the data for the first contract are not available.
(ii) The sample is based on trainer aircraft from 1938 to 1960. They comprise single-engine propeller-powered basic trainers of pre-World War II vintage (e.g. Tiger Moth); multi-engine propeller-powered large trainer aircraft (e.g. Oxford, Varsity); and jet-powered trainers (e.g. Meteor, Vampire, Canberra, Hunter, Lightning). Aircraft names show the company name first (e.g. de Havilland is the name of the company).
(iii) Aircraft are airframes only.
Source: DSTL (2010).

13.2 Cost Escalation on Trainers

Typically, cost escalation is associated with advanced combat aircraft, both fighters and bombers. Questions arise as to whether cost escalation arises with other groups of aircraft such as various types of trainer aircraft comprising basic, advanced and multi-engine types. Cost escalation factors are estimated for a group of propeller-powered basic trainer aircraft, except for the Jet Provost, which is included in the group as it was also a basic trainer (reflecting

Table 17 Cost escalation for trainer aircraft

Date	Quantity	Unit price (£) (constant June 1960 prices)	Real cost escalation factor
Miles Magister: June 1938	90	4,215	–
Miles Master: September 1940	500	15,542	x3.70
Percival Proctor: May 1943	512	3,609	–0.23
Percival Prentice: November 1945	5	15,374	x4.30
Boulton Paul Balliol: February 1947	20	34,164	x2.20
Percival Provost: August 1953	200	20,945	–0.61
Jet Provost: July 1957	100	17,276	–0.82
Airspeed Oxford: May 1938	136	9,770	NA
Wellington: December 1941	377	22,062	x2.30
Varsity: January 1952	60	67,878	x3.10

Notes:
(i) All trainers are arranged by date of the first contract, if available. Real cost escalation is the cost increase between generations of aircraft (e.g. cost increase from the Magister 1938 to the Magister 1940). Basic trainers are for the Magister through to the Jet Provost.
(ii) Quantities are for first production contract. Typically, first production contracts were for substantial numbers, but not for the Percival Prentice and the Balliol where later contracts were for substantial numbers.
(iii) Multi-engine trainers start with the Oxford followed by the Wellington and the Varsity.
(iv) For the Wellington, no details are available for the T10 so the data, including quantity, are based on the bomber version.

Source: DSTL (2010).

a shift to all jet trainers for the RAF). It can be seen that basic trainers showed both real cost *increases and decreases* (Table 17). Over the period 1938 to 1957 (almost twenty years), the real unit costs of basic trainer aircraft increased by a factor of slightly over 4.0. Cost escalation factors were considerably higher for jet-powered advanced trainer aircraft, reaching a factor of almost 11.0 over the thirteen-year period from 1947 to 1960 (see Table 17). Similarly, cost escalation was also estimated for multi-engine trainers between 1938 and 1952. Using a small sample, real cost escalation factors of between 2.3 and 3.1 were estimated for larger trainer aircraft. Overall, this section confirms that trainer aircraft were also subject to real cost escalation and that escalation is not confined to advanced combat aircraft.

14 Empirical Results

14.1 The Hypotheses

This section provides a further opportunity to test some of the hypotheses suggested by Augustine. Various rank correlations and regressions were estimated to test for Augustine weapons effects. Tests were undertaken of the determinants of unit prices for various types of aircraft.

First, for fighters and bomber aircraft, rank correlations were estimated between unit prices and each of weight, speed and time. Unit prices represented unit costs since military aircraft prices are usually estimated on the basis of unit production costs plus a profit margin. All price and unit costs were in constant prices (1959). Weight was all-up weight or the gross weight of an aircraft, measured in pounds (lb). Speed was aircraft speed in miles per hour (mph). For fighters and bomber aircraft, Spearman's rank correlation between unit prices and weight was +0.78, between unit prices and speed was +0.58 and between unit prices and time was +0.73, each showing positive and significant relationships between the variables. For fighters and bombers, greater weight and speed led to higher unit costs and higher unit prices, with real unit prices rising over time.

14.2 Regressions

Regressions were estimated for three different groups of aircraft, namely, fighters, fighters and bombers, and all combat aircraft, including large aircraft (Samples 1–3: time-series estimates). The results are summarised in Tables 18 and 19. Equation (1) in Table 18 (Sample 1) estimates unit prices for fighter aircraft against weight, speed and a linear time trend. The equation accounts for some 93 per cent of the variability in unit prices with significant coefficients for weight, speed and time (Equation (1), Table 18). However, the coefficient on time had an

Table 18 Empirical results: Sample 1 – UK fighter aircraft only ('R^2 [R squared]' indicates the coefficient of determination; 'DW' indicates 'Durbin Watson statistic')

Constant	Weight	Speed	Time	R^2	DW
(1) −50261.9 (−5.76)	5.527 (5.32)	93.052 (3.54)	−2829.3 (−2.205)	0.93	1.31
(2) −41995.5 (3.4)	6.53 (4.45)	–	−575.99 (−0.352)	0.85	1.56
(3) −46172.5 (−2.75)	–	131.24 (2.69)	1184.5 (0.59)	0.74	1.67

Notes: See notes to Table 20.

Table 19 Empirical results: Sample 2 – UK fighter and bomber aircraft ('R^2 [R squared]' indicates the coefficient of determination; 'DW' indicates 'Durbin Watson statistic')

Constant	Weight	Speed	Time	Dummy	R^2	DW
(4) −62665.8 (−2.87)	1.95 (4.94)	–	5542.6 (3.06)	–	0.72	1.26
(5) −75701.1 (−3.39)	2.52 (5.24)	138.91 (1.69)	375.5 (0.11)	–	0.74	1.39
(6) −67983.6 (2.35)	2.49 (4.42)	84.85 (1.55)	180.06 (0.05)	−1315.2 (0.43)	0.73	1.41
(7) −56257.5 (−1.86)	–	–	10175.3 (4.72)	–	0.45	0.89

Notes: See notes to Table 20.

unexpected negative sign. When the equation was re-estimated (Equation 2, Table 18) without the speed variable, it still resulted in a negative sign for time but this was not significant. Further estimates found speed significant, with a positive effect on unit prices for fighter aircraft (Equation (3), Table 18).

Different results for time emerged when the sample was widened to include both fighter and bomber aircraft (Sample 2). In the wider sample, both weight and time had significant and positive impacts on unit prices with the equations explaining over 70 per cent of the variations in unit prices (Table 19, Equations (4)–(7)). Elsewhere in Sample 2, the variables for speed and a dummy distinguishing between fighter and bomber aircraft were not statistically significant (Table 19, Equations (5) and (6)).

Overall, the empirical results found that aircraft weight was a major determinant of unit prices and there was some evidence of unit prices rising with time. Augustine found different results. He found prices rising with time and no impact on prices of aircraft characteristics such as weight and speed.

14.3 A Larger Sample

Finally, the sample was widened further to include large aircraft: Table 20 (n=38). The explanatory value of the equations with the larger sample was reduced substantially, explaining only some 30 per cent of price variations. Also, time was the only significant coefficient with the predicted positive coefficient: neither weight nor speed was significant, with the results confirming Augustine's original findings. Also, the Pearson correlation coefficient between unit prices and time was positive and significant,[4] confirming one of Augustine's predictions.

The empirical results presented in this section are exploratory, testing some of Augustine's hypotheses using time-series equations. Contrary to Augustine's findings of time as a significant factor, there was evidence that aircraft characteristics in the form of weight and speed were also statistically significant. Augustine claimed that unit costs were closely correlated with time rather than with changes in speed, weight or other technical parameters. Undoubtedly, there remains scope for much further work in this field.

15 A Critique

15.1 Characteristics of Augustine Weapons

Augustine weapons systems are characterised by the following features:

1. For advanced combat aircraft, rising unit costs correlate closely with the passage of time rather than with changes in speed, weight or other technical performance characteristics. According to Augustine, the trend of rising unit

---

[4] Some equations were estimated using a multiplicative form (log form). For the fighter and bomber sample (Sample 2, n=27), R^2 was estimated at 0.79 and significant and positive coefficients were estimated for weight and speed.

Table 20 Empirical results: Sample 3 – UK fighters, bombers and large aircraft ('R^2 [R squared]' indicates the coefficient of determination; 'DW' indicates 'Durbin Watson statistic')

Constant	Weight	Speed	Time	R^2	DW
(8)	0.911	–449.67	51588.3	0.311	1.12
–359788	(0.334)	(–0.84)	(2.79)		
(–1.67)					
(9)	1.883	–	41442.5	0.317	1.02
–446810	(0.765)		(2.995)		
(–2.39)					
(10)	–	–	47778.8	0.325	1.12
–451274.5			(4.33)		
(–2.43)					

Notes:
(i) The dependent variable in Tables 18–20 is the real unit price in pounds sterling in constant 1959 prices. Unit prices represent unit production costs with prices based on unit production costs plus a profit margin.
(ii) R^2 is adjusted for degrees of freedom. There was positive serial correlation in Table 19 Equations (4) and (7) and in Table 20, raising doubts about the reliability of the regression equations. Figures in brackets are t-ratios. In Table 18, Equations (1)–(3), coefficients for weight and speed are significant at the 1 per cent or 5 per cent levels. Similarly, in Table 19 t-ratios of 3 or over are significant at the 1 per cent level, and in Table 20 the coefficients for time were significant at the 1 per cent level.
(iii) W is all-up weight in pounds or gross weight if all-up weight data are not available; speed is in mph; and time trend is a linear trend starting with 1 in June 1934, based on the date of the first production contract or the earliest production contract depending on data availability. Finally, D is a dummy variable for fighter and bomber aircraft where 1 = fighter aircraft and 0 = bomber aircraft.
(iv) Fighter aircraft are based on n=13 comprising Gauntlet (June 1934), Gladiator (November 1937), Hurricane (September 1938), Spitfire (December 1939), Beaufighter (February 1942), Typhoon (July 1943), Tempest (October 1943), Meteor (December 1943), Vampire (February 1946), Venom (January 1953), Hunter (January 1955), Javelin (January 1957) and Lightning (April 1959).
(v) Bomber aircraft are based on n=14 comprising Whitley (February 1938), Hampden (August 1938), Blenheim (February 1939), Battle (October 1939), Stirling (June 1941), Wellington (November 1941), Halifax (June 1942), Mosquito (August 1943), Lancaster (January 1944), Lincoln (February 1946), Canberra (June 1951), Vulcan (December 1954), Victor (May 1955) and Valiant (September 1955). In brackets are the month and year of the first production contract.
(vi) There were three UK samples: Sample 1 was UK fighter aircraft only (n=13); Sample 2 was UK fighter and bomber aircraft over the period 1934 to 1959 (n=27); Sample 3 was all UK aircraft comprising fighters, bombers and large aircraft consisting of transports plus maritime patrol aircraft (n=38). Figures are rounded.

Source: DSTL (2010).

costs also applies to commercial aircraft, helicopters, ships, tanks, automobiles and homes, but at a lower growth rate: a factor of 2.0 every ten years.
2. Cost and budget trends led Augustine to forecast that by 2054 the entire US defence budget will purchase just one aircraft. Similarly, the UK will reach the single-aircraft position almost two years before the USA.
3. Rising costs reflect the use of complex electronics, computer software and the growing application of stealth technologies which open up vast new capability vistas which are then crammed into each new generation of a product.
4. The engineering mindset of decision-makers in the military industrial complex values technology for technology's sake, regardless of its cost effectiveness. Critics claim that major weapons systems are laden with technological 'bells and whistles' which add considerably to costs but little to military effectiveness.

15.2 Correlations and Causation

A starting point in critiquing Augustine is that much of his analysis is based on extrapolating historical cost data, which presents the possibility of confusing observed trends with causation. Correlations are not evidence of causation. The problem with trends is that they bend: there is a famous saying that a trend is a trend but the question is will it bend and alter its course through some unforeseen force and come to a premature end! The possible end cannot be ignored for Augustine systems.

Augustine cost extrapolations have been used by critics of the military industrial complex as proof of wasteful military spending, gold plating and defence establishments with little incentive to control costs. They claim that military investment is captured by complex vested interests within the MIPC and that much new defence capability is over-engineered and wasteful, leading to smaller quantities of increasingly complex and costlier equipment. Nor do we focus on the benefits side of military investment, examining whether these ever costlier Augustine investments lead to more defence being produced by each incremental dollar. Here, there is a major deficiency: there is an absence of a money value of defence output. Instead, typically defence output is measured by inputs and the assumption that inputs equal outputs. On this basis all increases in defence inputs mean higher defence outputs, which is a far from satisfactory position!

15.3 Lack of a Theory

There remains a major deficiency, namely, that the Augustine approach lacks a well-established theory in the form of a set of definitions and assumptions which provide logical deductions explaining behaviour. Instead, there are assertions and anecdotal evidence which provide a good story but do not represent a well-established theory. Augustine's 'model' comprises a set of observations which have been joined together to form a narrative which is appealing and attractive but by itself does not form a theory.

16 Future Challenges

16.1 Balance between Augustine Weapons and Cheap Drones

What are the implications of Augustine weapons for the future of defence industries and the armed forces? The high-technology feature of Augustine weapons will lead to a smaller number of larger firms which will be R&D-intensive rather than production-intensive. The search for markets and production orders probably means more international mergers. But these trends will be offset by the emergence of small and cheap drones that are capable of a variety of military tasks. For example, drones might be used for surveillance and observation, thus replacing the military personnel traditionally used for such tasks. They also provide a long-range strike capability, so enabling remote warfare (e.g. the ability to hit targets without military occupation of the country). But with cheap drones there will be pressures to make them more complex so as to perform ever-more-complex tasks at ever-increasing costs: ultimately, they will become as costly as Augustine weapons.

So, where is the likely balance between expensive Augustine weapons and cheap drones? Currently, there is a role for both. Substitution effects might lead to cheap drones replacing costly Augustine weapons. Alternatively, drones and Augustine weapons might be complementary, with costly Augustine weapons controlling a number of drones in a range of strike and reconnaissance missions. The model here is swarms of cheap drones commanded by costly Augustine weapons (the USA created Unit X as part of the Pentagon to establish links with Silicon Valley and transform the future of war: Shah and Kirchhoff, 2024).

Both Augustine weapons and drones have impacts on the armed forces. Costly high-technology Augustine weapons mean smaller numbers, with capital and technology replacing military personnel. Already, some nations are finding it too costly to replace their combat aircraft fleets and have chosen to opt out of maintaining combat air capabilities (e.g. New Zealand). There are implications for the training of military personnel, with probably a greater reliance on the use of simulators for training. High costs mean greater incentives for national armed forces to share such weapons, creating *international* military forces and capabilities. The emergence of cheap drones creates opposite trends to the Augustine effects. Like Augustine weapons, they are technology-intensive, but their relative cheapness means that they can be purchased in large numbers. There will be substitution effects for the armed forces as drones replace some of the traditional roles undertaken by manned systems (e.g. strike and reconnaissance missions). Training requirements in the armed forces will change as military personnel use computers to acquire skills compared with traditional battlefield experience. Skilled labour will be in greater demand as military personnel will need to be more skilled to cope with complex equipment. Future demands for military personnel will be for highly skilled inputs and there will be concerns about the armed forces obtaining a worthwhile return on their costly training investments (Arce, 2023).

16.2 International Collaboration

The continually rising costs of Augustine weapons create greater pressures for international collaboration to share costly development and combine small production orders. The costs of Augustine weapons means that they are tailor-made for international collaboration. For example, currently European nations are developing two types of future combat aircraft, namely, the UK-led Tempest forming the Global Combat Aircraft Programme, comprising the UK, Italy and Japan, with an in-service date of 2035 and the Franco-German-Spanish sixth-generation fighter aircraft.[5] Questions arise as to whether these nations can afford to develop two similar independent projects to be bought in small numbers. Whilst international collaboration is economically attractive, it has political costs: who will be the project leader and how will work be shared between the partner nations?

International collaboration benefits both development and production work. Development work is a fixed cost which can be shared between two or more nations. For example, consider a project with development costs of £20 billion: without collaboration a single nation would pay the fixed cost of £20 billion, but shared among four nations the bill for each nation is only £5 billion (*ceteris paribus*). Similarly, sharing production work has benefits. Each nation might demand, say, 100 aircraft; a four-nation collaboration would therefore mean a production order for 400 aircraft rather than the 100 aircraft required by one nation, and an order for 400 aircraft results in lower unit costs from economies of scale and learning.

But this simple economics of collaboration suffers from one flaw: the *ceteris paribus* assumption. With international collaboration, other things do not remain unchanged and the assumption of fixed development costs remaining unchanged at £20 billion is most likely to be null and void. Nations will have

---

[5] In 2024 the UK, Italy and Japan created an international organisation to oversee the aircraft's development.

their national requirements for an advanced technology project and each will demand to be involved in the advanced technology part of the programme (e.g. fuselage, engine, avionics) and to get their 'fair share' of the work. As a result, the work share or 'fair shares' requirement is likely to depart from efficiency criteria. For example, each nation will demand a flight test centre and a final assembly line and similar duplication will arise in the management of the collaboration. An official UK report on the collaborative Typhoon programme concluded that collaborative decision-making was inefficient (NAO, 2011). These are not costless additions to the collaboration and will increase total development costs beyond the original £20 billion used in this example. But international collaboration will continue to be economically worthwhile so long as its costs are less than the costs of an independent national development (in this example, £20 billion). Or collaboration is worthwhile so long as it costs less than the costs of importing from the least cost foreign supplier. In these circumstances, cost–benefit analysis can be applied. But judgement cannot be avoided, especially in valuing the costs and benefits of the intangible elements such as national independence and the timescale of the assessment. Cost estimates will vary and be subject to different degrees of reliability. For example, cost estimates at the start of a project will be less reliable than later estimates, though often initial cost estimates are used as the basis for a project decision.

The Airbus A400M airlifter is a good example of an international collaboration involving a large number of nations. Initially, it was expected that Airbus as a successful civil airliner firm would have few problems in developing a military airlifter. Reality was different. The airlifter was a seven-nation development using a new engine and composite technologies. Since its launch in 2003 it has been characterised by cost overruns and considerable delays. Costs have risen by about €8 billion on a project originally expected to cost €20 billion and the first aircraft was delivered four years late. It has also failed to meet its capability requirements, leading to further penalties. The original contract assumed wrongly that commercial terms could be applied to a complex international military aircraft procurement. Problems remain with the engine and the gearbox and Airbus admits that it under-estimated the complexity of the A400M.

For the future, the next development in technology might well be the development of space forces with the capability of destroying communications and surveillance satellites. Such satellites provide information to Earth-based armed forces, so their destruction would provide potential enemies with a battle-winning advantage (Markowski et al., 2023).

16.3 Role of Humans

There is a further factor which cannot be ignored, namely, the role of human beings in Augustine weapons. Despite their massive complexity, such weapons are still operated and commanded by humans with all their limitations: humans, unlike popes, are not infallible. Artificial intelligence (AI) means the emergence of different types of military commander – AI commanders – having available vast amounts of data for their decision-making. Machines will support human decisions and might even replace them by making decisions. An example illustrates the possibilities. In 1940, Fighter Command managed the Battle of Britain with radar, ground spotters and command centres which alerted aircraft to the threats from the attacking force. Today, the Israeli Iron Dome air defence system manages air defence without human intervention: the trajectory of incoming rockets is tracked and only those likely to reach important targets are selected for interception. The system is currently expensive; the costs of each interception are high, although the attacking drones and rockets themselves are relatively inexpensive (Freedman, 2023). Using AI means that decisions will not be dominated by inter-service rivalries and personalities (e.g. Montgomery and Patton in World War II); however, such disputes and differences in judgement are sure to occur in different forms.

16.4 Communications

Military communications also remain important. The ability to communicate quickly and accurately with military staff in different locations will continue to be important even with Augustine weapons. And communications have been subject to technical change, varying from the historical examples of communications depending on human runners taking messages between command centres to flag signals between ships and the use of pigeons! Communication failures have determined the outcomes of battles (e.g. Arnhem). Modern military communications are much more complex, involving computers, information technology, networks and space-based satellites, and these systems need to be protected (cyber security). Allocating Augustine weapons in battlefield situations will depend on communications. Costly Augustine weapons can be destroyed by faulty communications; the systems are so costly that they might require even costlier systems for their protection!

16.5 The Future

What of the future for Augustine weapons? Futures are characterised by uncertainty: today's winners are tomorrow's losers. New technology has dominated military weapons and some technical change has been revolutionary as well as evolutionary. The jet engine is an example of revolutionary technical change rendering obsolescent many previous engine technologies. Most defence equipment is made to order; thus, for military firms to develop and produce the capabilities needed for Augustine weapons, the risks will be largely shifted to taxpayers. This creates new regulatory problems, which will be international as firms increasingly seek international mergers, and there will be new opportunities for rent seeking. All of this suggests that taxpayers will be at even greater risk of exploitation by the MIPC.

Augustine weapons are costly and will become costlier. But they are procured against a background where wars are also costly. The costs of war are direct and indirect. Direct costs include deaths and injury amongst military and civilian personnel for all the participants. There are also costs to physical structures in the destruction and damage to buildings, homes and infrastructure (e.g. roads, railways and bridges). Air strikes will affect populations in terms of their location, movement and shelter. The costs become greater where a population is invaded and subdued. Invasion means a loss of freedoms and liberty, resulting in starvation and slavery. The Nazi German occupation of Europe and the Soviet Union in World War II is a good example. Once the costs of war are considered, expensive Augustine weapons might be regarded as worthwhile: they are cheap at the price.

Augustine weapons are not unique. The term applies to current weapons, but there are historical examples. Castles are the medieval equivalent. They were costly and at the time were superior, battle-winning weapons. But new technology in the form of cannons rendered them obsolete; and in the military field, new technologies are always emerging. Previous generations of battleships were the Augustine weapons of their day, but along came aircraft and aircraft carriers, which rendered them obsolescent with nuclear weapons having similar effects. Regardless of the age, all weapons have one distinctive characteristic: they are designed to kill people. Augustine weapons have a special added characteristic in that they are much costlier than their predecessors.

17 Overall Conclusions

1. Augustine's original contribution was to highlight that weapons are costly and becoming costlier, with rising costs meaning fewer being bought. His famous forecast was a single-aircraft air force by 2054. Others have widened the forecast to a future defence force of a single-warship navy, a single-tank army and Starship Enterprise for the air force.

2. Augustine found that fighter aircraft unit costs have risen by a factor of 4.0 every ten years, with rising unit costs closely correlated with the passage of time. Few aircraft in this study corresponded to the strict Augustine hypothesis of unit costs rising by a factor of 4.0 every ten years, although there were problems in obtaining data on this hypothesis.
3. A major source of rising unit costs is electronics and software.
4. The rising costs of Augustine weapons are explained by the behaviour of agents in the military–industrial–political complex. These comprise political parties, bureaucracies and producer groups.
5. The study addresses two questions. First, do aircraft show evidence of intergenerational cost escalation? Second, is there evidence of decreasing unit costs? The answers are that the study found considerable evidence in real terms of unit cost escalation embracing fighter, bomber, transport and trainer aircraft. For fighters the median real cost escalation factor is 1.3 and for bombers it is higher at 1.7. There is also considerable evidence of aircraft as a decreasing cost industry and evidence of learning economies.
6. Cost escalation is not confined to military aerospace projects; it is also found on a range of civil and private sector projects.
7. Our empirical results confirm the importance of time in explaining unit price variations.
8. Future trends are explored for defence industries and the armed forces. Defence industries are likely to be smaller, with more international mergers and international companies, and thus even greater problems of regulating the industry. The armed forces will become more skill-intensive, facing challenges in obtaining a return on their costly training investments.

Statistical Appendices

There are two appendices. Appendix I presents examples which support and reinforce the data shown in the main text. It shows pre-World War II aircraft in the form of the Hind, the Sunderland flying boat, the Whitley, the Hampden and the Battle, as well as famous World War II aircraft, namely, the Hurricane, the Halifax and the Mosquito. It also shows post-1945 aircraft in the form of the Vampire, the Venom and the Javelin jet fighters, plus jet bombers, namely, the two V-bombers, the Victor and the Vulcan. Appendix II provides a case study of actual data used for the pricing of the Canberra jet bomber in 1953.

Appendix I: Supplementary Data

Appendix I shows pre-World War II aircraft beginning with the Hind followed by World War II aircraft and then post-1945 aircraft. The appendix supplements data in the main text.

The Hind bomber showed decreasing costs typically in the region of 10 per cent for increased output. Profit rates were unchanged at 10 per cent.

Short Sunderland: Flying Boat

This was a unique and iconic aircraft, with a first production contract in early 1937. It is different in being a flying boat. Data on unit prices are shown in Table A2. There were four production sites, at Rochester, Lake Windermere, Belfast and Blackburn (Dumbarton factory). Unit prices for early production contracts show the costs of entry for alternative suppliers, with Rochester the least cost supplier. In 1937, profit rates on the Sunderland were 10 per cent, but by 1943–44 rates had fallen to 2–4 per cent. Total output was 749 aircraft. The data on unit costs are misleading and do not reflect actual unit prices; for example, data for the Rochester contracts show rising unit prices to early 1942 but a reduction for the whole period 1937 to 1944.

Unit costs for the Whitley bomber fell substantially over the contract, especially for unit production and unit labour costs. For example, the November 1942 unit labour costs were some 30 per cent of their 1938 level. Profit rates also declined towards the end of the contract.

The Hampden was a decreasing cost aircraft across all dimensions, but especially for unit labour costs, which almost halved over the production run. Profit margins also fell with volume.

Statistical Appendices

Table A1 Hind bomber

Date	Quantity	Unit price (£)	Unit production cost (£)	Unit labour cost (£)	Profit margin (%)
3/1937	20	1,925	1,644	440	10.0
3/1937	244	1,718	1,537	384	10.0

Note: Two contracts were awarded in March 1937. All are in constant March 1937 prices. All cost data in the appendices and the main study are for airframes only.
Source: DSTL (2010).

Table A2 Sunderland flying boat

Date	Unit price (£)	Percentage change (%)
Rochester: 3/1937	43,535	–
Rochester: 9/1944	38,863	89.0
Lake Windermere: 3/1942	51,830	–
Windermere: 1/1944	46,260	89.0
Belfast: 8/1944	53,200	–
Belfast: 2/1947	39,055	73.0
Blackburn: 4/1944	124,277	–
Blackburn: 11/1944	41,596	33.0

Notes:
(i) All data are in constant June 1947 prices except for Lake Windermere contracts, which are in constant January 1944 prices.
(ii) Percentage change shows the price reduction between the first and the last contracts (e.g. between Rochester's 1937 and 1944 contracts).
(iii) Named sites show the location of production work.
(iv) Unit prices comprise unit costs and a profit margin.
Source: DSTL (2010).

Table A3 Armstrong Whitworth Whitley heavy bomber

Date	Quantity	Unit price (£)	Unit production cost (£)	Unit labour cost (£)	Profit margin (%)
2/1938	first 10	41,537	27,305	13,493	7.5
11/1942	150	17,900	6,789	3,750	3.5

Note: Contracts are in constant November 1942 prices.
Source: DSTL (2010).

Table A4 Handley Page Hampden

Date	Quantity	Unit price (£)	Unit production cost (£)	Unit labour cost (£)	Profit margin (%)
8/1938	180	14,061	12,273	3,913	8.0
6/1941	120	9,350	8,920	2,049	5.0

Note: All data are in constant June 1941 prices.
Source: DSTL (2010).

Table A5 Fairey Battle

Date	Quantity	Unit price (£)	Unit production cost (£)	Unit labour cost (£)	Profit margin (%)
11/1938	155	26,631	24,068	8,806	7.5
10/1940	110	5,983	5,307	910	6.0

Note: Prices are constant at October 1940.
Source: DSTL (2010).

The Battle showed decreasing costs with major reductions for unit labour costs, which in 1940 were 10 per cent of the 1938 levels. Again, profit margins declined with volume.

Bristol Blenheim: Bomber

The Blenheim is a decreasing cost aircraft, with unit labour costs in 1941 at some 14% of their 1939 level. Profits declined with output.

Hawker Hurricane Fighter

The Hurricane is clearly a decreasing cost aircraft. Cost–quantity data for the production of the Hurricane between 1938 and 1944 (first and last contracts) are shown in Table A7. Between the start and final contracts, unit prices and costs declined by 30 per cent and labour costs fell by over 50 per cent. Profit margins also declined from over 7 per cent in 1938 to around 4 per cent in 1942 and to 3 per cent for the final contract.

Short Stirling: Heavy Bomber

The Stirling is one of three World War II heavy bombers. The other two were the Halifax and the Lancaster. The cost data for the Stirling were in varied forms and were not fully available and reported. However, the limited data available show the

Table A6 Blenheim

Date	Quantity	Unit price (£)	Unit production cost (£)	Unit labour cost (£)	Profit margin (%)
2/1939	10	25,488	23,361	8,688	7.5
11/1941	190	6,912	5,807	1,218	6.0

Note: All data are in constant November 1941 prices.
Source: DSTL (2010).

Table A7 Hurricane fighter aircraft

Date	Quantity	Unit price (£)	Unit production cost (£)	Unit labour cost (£)	Profit margin (%)
12/1938	518	5,763	6,104	1,282	7.4
6/1944	267	4,093	4,275	598	3.0

Note: All prices are in June 1944 prices: this was the date of the final contract.
Source: DSTL (2010).

Stirling as a decreasing cost aircraft. In June 1941, the unit price was £44,990 (1948 prices), but by May 1948 it had fallen to £19,000, which was some 42 per cent of its 1941 level. Price fixing for World War II aircraft was delayed and the May 1948 price agreement was for aircraft delivered between 1943 and 1945.

Handley Page Halifax: Heavy Bomber

The Halifax bomber shows decreasing prices and costs. Between 1942 and 1946, Handley Page unit prices halved whilst unit production and unit labour costs declined by some 30 per cent and 40 per cent, respectively. Interestingly, the cost data for Handley Page showed unit price and costs rising for the final two contracts, suggesting adverse productivity effects as labour reacted to the ending of production work (tailing-off effects). No similar effect was observed for the contracts for English Electric's work on the Halifax. Profit rates also declined with larger quantities, from 5 per cent for early contracts to lower rates of 1.5 per cent to 3.5 per cent for later contracts.[6] Table A8 also shows comparative price and cost data for the original developer of the Halifax and English Electric as a second supplier. For the early production contracts, English Electric was the

---

[6] For Handley Page, profits decreased to 2.5 per cent in 1943, 1.5 per cent in 1945, 2.5 per cent in March 1946 and 3 per cent in July 1946. Profit rates for English Electric declined from 5 per cent in April 1942 to 3.5 per cent in October 1942 and remained at that level till the end of the contract in 1945.

Table A8 Halifax bomber

Date	Quantity	Unit price (£)	Unit production cost (£)	Unit labour cost (£)	Profit margin (%)
HP 6/1942	20	42,300	NA	NA	5.0
HP 6/1942	next 180	30,900	11,300	6,200	5.0
HP 7/1946	final 150	20,600	8,000	3,700	2.5
	Total 1,437				
EE 4/1942	first 25	38,200	21,800	10,700	5.0
EE 4/1942	next 25	32,400	16,400	8,000	5.0
EE 1/1945	final 350	15,000	5,700	2,800	3.5
	Total 2,470				

Notes:
(i) Data show unit prices and costs for first production contracts and final contracts at the dates and quantities shown. None of the other observations between the first and the final contracts are shown.
(ii) Prices and unit costs are in constant July 1946 prices based on the date of the final contract. Costs are for airframe only.
(iii) Data are for two major contractors, namely, Handley Page (HP), the original developer, and English Electric (EE), a second supplier. First contracts include the cost of jigs and tools, but these costs are not included in final contracts.
(iv) Data for output show production numbers ordered at the date of contract. For example, HP received the first production order for 200 aircraft in June 1942 with cost data shown for the first 20 aircraft and for the next 180 aircraft. Its final order was in July 1946, for 150 aircraft from a total production run of 1,437 aircraft awarded to the company. Similarly, English Electric received a final order for 350 aircraft from a total output of 2,470 aircraft from the company.
(v) NA is not available.

Source: DSTL (2010).

higher cost supplier, but the competitive position reversed at the end of the contracts. English Electric's final price–cost position reflected learning economies from its larger cumulative output compared with that of Handley Page.

de Havilland Mosquito: Light Bomber

The de Havilland Mosquito was a unique World War II combat aircraft constructed from wood.[7] It had a different unit cost curve which was not smooth; it sloped continually downwards over its initial production, but then there was

---

[7] It comprised bought-out parts, raw materials, subcontracts and spruce, which together formed 73 per cent of its unit price.

Statistical Appendices

Table A9 de Havilland Mosquito

Date	Quantity	Unit price (£)	Unit production cost (£)	Unit labour cost (£)	Profit margin (%)
DH 8/1943	first 50 *of 2,370*	14,922	3,353	1,295	3.0
DH 8/1948	51	12,600	1,178	357	5.0
SM 1/1944	800	19,498	9,608	4,597	2.3
SM 9/1945	265	8,997	2,972	1,454	4.0
P 8/1944	first 20 *of 250*	14,269	12,824	1,623	2.6
	last 150 *of 250*	9,864	8,953	649	2.6

Notes:
(i) All data are in constant prices based on the date of the final contract for de Havilland (August 1948).
(ii) de Havilland (DH) was the original developer for the Mosquito; Standard Motors (SM) and Percival (P) were alternative suppliers for it.
(iii) Unit prices and costs are based on early production contracts. For de Havilland, data are for the first 50 aircraft from a contract for 2,370 aircraft.

Source: DSTL (2010).

a generally level stretch ending in a jagged-toothed section (not shown in Table A9). Overall, unit prices, production costs and labour costs declined between the initial output and the final output.

Both Standard Motors and Percival were new entrants and higher cost suppliers for both unit production and unit labour costs compared with the original developer (de Havilland). Both showed decreasing costs for unit prices, production costs and labour costs, but Standard Motors showed much greater percentage reductions than Percival.

de Havilland Vampire Aircraft

Table A10 shows detailed unit cost data for a series of batch contracts for the Vampire fighter bomber aircraft; each batch is for 10–20 aircraft. The batches are from the same cost curve at the same date so we can be confident about unit prices and costs being from the same curve; however, they are not necessarily X-efficient points. The data confirm classic decreasing cost curves for all price and cost categories. For example, unit prices and unit production costs at units 101–120 were some 21 per cent of the prices for units 1–5, and the unit labour costs at units 101–120 were just 16 per cent of the labour costs for units 1–5.

Table A10 Vampire cost curves

Quantity	Unit price (£)	Unit production cost (£)	Unit labour cost (£)
1–5	29,000	27,359	9,625
6–10	18,890	17,800	6,062
11–20	17,730	16,727	5,625
21–40	14,915	14,070	4,875
41–60	12,430	11,725	3,937
61–80	9,615	9,070	2,875
81–100	6,800	6,412	1,812
101–120	6,130	5,787	1,562

Notes:
(i) The contract at February 1946 is for Mark 1 F2. Profit rate is 6 per cent for all batches,
(ii) Output range is 1–120 aircraft.
(iii) Overheads are at 150 per cent, but unit costs exclude jigs and tools.
(iv) The contract was with English Electric, which manufactured most de Havilland Vampire aircraft. Owing to wartime pressures for existing types of aircraft at de Havilland, the majority of the Vampire aircraft were produced by English Electric.

Source: DSTL (2010).

Table A11 shows price and cost data for a different version of the Vampire, namely, the trainer aircraft. Trainers involved higher unit prices and costs compared with the Mark 1 aircraft, confirming that cost curves varied with different types of aircraft (Table A10). Unit prices and production costs declined between 1953 and 1954 but unit labour costs rose over this period. After December 1954 unit prices rose. There is also evidence of learning economies 'tapering off' towards the end of the production line. Interestingly, unit profitability shows some rise towards the end of the contract (Table A11).

de Havilland Venom: Fighter

The Venom was a development of the Vampire but, surprisingly, its unit cost curves are different from the general trends for most aircraft in the sample. Its unit cost curve declined for the early output levels (to 260 units) and then followed a rising trend with local 'jagged' peaks and troughs. A partial explanation of these unit cost features might have been that the unit costs were for drastically different aircraft, namely, fighter bombers and night fighters (which included radars: Table A12). It is noticeable that profitability increased towards the end of the production run.

Table A11 Unit costs for Vampire trainer aircraft

Date	Quantity	Unit price (£)	Unit production cost (£)	Unit labour cost (£)	Profitability (%)
5/1953	50	23,723	19,971	2,975	5.0
12/1954	135	19,850	18,650	3,200	6.5
12/1954	20	20,407	NA	NA	NA
6/1955	66	21,500	NA	NA	NA
6/1955	24	22,500	NA	NA	NA

Notes:
(i) In some instances, two contracts were awarded for different quantities in the same month.
(ii) NA is data not available. Data are in constant June 1955 prices. Costs of jigs and tools are not included in trainer contracts.
(iii) Contracts for December 1954 are for Mark 22 (order of twenty aircraft); all other contracts are for Mark 11. The contract at June 1955 is taken as the date of the final contract.
Source: DSTL (2010).

Table A12 Venom unit cost curve

Date	Quantity	Unit price (£)	Unit production cost (£)	Unit labour cost (£)	Profitability (%)
1/1953	60	23,370	20,678	2,343	5.0
7/1956	123	35,560	30,988	4,774	6.5

Notes:
(i) Unit prices and costs are in July 1956 prices.
(ii) Outputs were for different marks of aircraft, including Marks 1 and 4 and night fighter Marks 2 and 3.
Source: DSTL (2010).

Gloster Javelin: All-Weather Fighter

The cost data for the Javelin show output in different batches over 100 units. Javelin price and unit cost data show decreasing costs over the first 100 units with substantial reductions for unit labour cost. Unit prices and production costs at 100 units were about 50 per cent of their level at 1–20 units and labour costs at 100 units were some 44 per cent of their level at 1–20 units. Unit profitability remained unchanged with higher output.

Table A13 Unit costs for Javelin

Date	Quantity	Unit price (£)	Unit production cost (£)	Unit labour cost (£)	Profitability (%)
1/1957	1–20	150,400	139,900	121,500	7.5
1/1957	20–30	104,800	97,500	79,100	7.5
1/1957	30–50	87,800	81,700	63,300	7.5
1/1957	50–100	77,100	71,700	53,300	7.5

Notes
(i) Costs do not include jigs and tools. Unit labour costs include overheads.
(ii) All prices and costs are in constant January 1957 prices.
(iii) Total output for the January 1957 contract was 200 units.
Source: DSTL (2010).

Table A14 Victor bomber

Date	Quantity	Unit price (£)	Unit production cost (£)	Unit labour cost (£)	Unit profit (%)
5/1955	33	244,000	232,400	54,040	5.0
12/1955	21	248,700	NA	NA	NA
12/1956	25	813,000 (first five) 501,000 (next twenty)	564,000	NA	6.0
1/1958	30	408,000	374,000	74,700	9.0

Notes:
(i) Price and cost data are in constant January 1958 prices, without the costs of jigs and tools.
(ii) NA is not available.
(iii) Unit production cost for December 1956 is an average of the data for the first five and the next twenty aircraft.
(iv) Total production was 109 aircraft over four contracts from May 1955 to January 1958.
Source: DSTL (2010).

Handley Page Victor: Heavy Bomber

Unit prices and cost data for the Victor do not show any sign of decreasing over any of its production contracts (Table A14). Instead, prices and costs rose and

Table A15 Vulcan bomber

Date	Quantity	Unit price (£)	Unit production cost (£)	Unit labour cost (£)	Unit profit (%)
12/1954	62	340,000	314,200	60,700	8.0
1/1956	24	285,000	NA	NA	NA
4/1956	8	268,000	NA	NA	NA
10/1957	40	400,000	NA	200,000 (including overheads)	10.0

Notes:
(i) The contract for December 1954 was in two parts and figures shown are based on averages for the two contracts.
(ii) NA is not available.
(iii) Jigs and tools are excluded.
(iv) Contracts for two prototype aircraft are not shown.
(v) All prices and costs are in October 1957 constant prices.
Source: DSTL (2010).

then fell. Profitability also rose with greater output, rising from 5 per cent at the start of production to 9 per cent at the end of the contract.

Avro Vulcan: Heavy Bomber

The price and cost data in Table A15 show declining unit prices over the initial output but substantial rising prices and costs for the final contract. Unit prices at April 1956 are about 80 per cent of their 1954 levels. Profitability is higher for the final contract. Interestingly, the unit profitability for the Vulcan is higher at the end of the contract and is also higher than for the Victor.

In general, the Appendix I evidence shows aircraft as a decreasing cost activity, especially for pre-World War II and World War II aircraft. The exceptions are for the more recent post-1945 jet aircraft where production runs are considerably smaller (Venom, Victor and Vulcan).

Appendix II: Example of Contract Pricing for Canberra Jet Bombers, 1953

This appendix shows how prices are actually determined. Table A16 shows the actual contract used to price two orders for Canberra jet bombers in February 1953. The contracts were priced on the basis of average costs plus a profit margin, with the final price including an allowance for jigs and tools for each aircraft.

Table A16 Pricing case study: The Canberra bomber, 1953

Unit cost item (£)	Canberra PR Mk 3 (Q = 34)	Canberra T Mk 4 (Q = 8)
Labour	11,368	12,030
Overheads	22,559	23,804
Materials	14,891	15,009
Flight tests	585	585
Others	3,089	3,089
Subtotal	*52,492*	*54,507*
Profit: 5% (approx.)	2,508	2,543
Unit price	55,000	57,050
Jigs and tools	4,500	4,500
Final price	**59,500**	**61,550**

Notes:
(i) PR is photo reconnaissance; T is trainer aircraft; Q is quantity ordered for each contract.
(ii) All costs are in current February 1953 prices, with contracts agreed in February 1953. Costs are costs per unit or average costs. Delivery is from November 1952 to November 1953 for PR versions and from April 1953 to August 1953 for trainers.
(iii) Other costs include Rolls-Royce charges, drawings, extra costs of sub-contracting and head office expenses.
(iv) Overhead recovery rates varied between 198 per cent and 228 per cent. Jigs and tools costs were £2,500–£5,000 per aircraft, but on some batches for Avro they were £75,000 per aircraft and for some Short Bros batches they reached £90,000 per aircraft.

Source: DSTL (2010).

Table A16 shows labour, overheads and materials costs forming over 80 per cent of the final price of the Canberra. Overhead costs were 37–39 per cent of the final price, material costs were about 25 per cent and labour costs almost 20 per cent of the final price. Profit rates were 5 per cent on costs.

References

Amann, D. (2022). Changing Path and Curbing Cost Escalation: Lessons Learnt from the Gripen Case. *Defence and Peace Economics*, 33(4), 421–437.

Arce, D. (2023). Cybersecurity for Defence Economists. *Defence and Peace Economics*, 34(6), 705–725.

Arena, M. V., Blickstein, I., Younossi, O., and Grammich, C. A. (2006). *Why Has the Cost of Navy Ships Risen? A Macroscopic Examination of the Trends in US Navy Ship Costs over the Past Several Decades*. RAND, Santa Monica, CA.

Arena, M. V., Younossi, O., Brancato, K., Blickstein, I., and Grammich, C. A. (2008). *Why Has the Cost of Fixed-Wing Aircraft Risen?* RAND, Santa Monica, CA.

Augustine, N. R. (1987). *Augustine's Laws*. Penguin, London.

Baloff, N. (1966). The Learning Curve – Some Controversial Issues. *Journal of Industrial Economics*, XIV(3), 275–282.

Brauer, J., and van Tuyll, H. (2008). *Castles, Battles and Bombs*. University of Chicago Press, Chicago, IL.

CRS (2021). *Air Force B-21 Raider Long Range Strike Bomber*. Congressional Research Service, US Congress, Washington, DC.

CRS (2023). *Navy Virginia (SSN-774) Class Attack Submarine Procurement: Background and Issues for Congress*. O'Rourke, R. Congressional Research Service, US Congress, Washington, DC.

CRS (2024). *Navy Ford Class Aircraft Carrier Programme*. Congressional Research Service, February, Washington, DC.

Davies, N., Eager, A., Maier, M., and Penfold, L. (2011). *Intergenerational Equipment Cost Escalation*. Ministry of Defence, London.

DSTL (2010). *Historical Cost Data of RAF Aircraft, 1935–1965*. Ministry of Defence using DSTL version. Ministry of Defence, London. The author made extensive corrections to the data to convert to constant prices using the UK Retail Price Index 1987 = 100 and other changes, so creating a unique and original data set.

Freedman, L. (2023). *Command: The Politics of Military Operations from Korea to Ukraine*. Penguin, London.

Hartley, K., and Cubitt, J. (1976–77). *Cost Escalation in the UK*. The Civil Service, Expenditure Committee, Appendix 44, House of Commons Paper535-III, Session 1976/77.

Hartley, K. (2017). UK Defence Inflation and Cost Escalation, in Hartley, K., and Solomon, B. (eds.), *Defence Inflation* (ch. 3). Routledge, Abingdon.

(Originally published in the April 2016 issue of *Defence and Peace Economics*, 27(2), 184–207.)

Hartley, K. (2023). Costs and Prices of UK Military Aircraft in War and Peace. *Defence and Peace Economics*, 34(4), 512–526.

Hartley, K., and Sandler, T. (eds.) (2001). *The Economics of Defence*. Elgar Reference Collection vol. 3. Edward Elgar, Cheltenham.

HC755 (2011). *Management of Typhoon Project*. National Audit Office, London.

Hartley, K., and Solomon, B. (eds.) (2017). *Defence Inflation*. Routledge, Abingdon.

Hove, K., and Lillekvelland, T. (2017). Investment Cost Escalation: An Overview of the Literature and Revised Estimates, in Hartley, K., and Solomon, B. (eds.), *Defence Inflation* (ch. 4). Routledge, Abingdon. (Originally published in the April 2016 issue of *Defence and Peace Economics*, 27(2), 208–230.)

ICE (2018). *Reducing the Gap between Cost Estimates and Outturns for Major Infrastructure Projects and Programmes*. Institute of Civil Engineers, London.

IPA (2021). *Cost Estimating Guidance*. Infrastructure and Projects Authority, London.

Johnstone, B. M. (2020). *Augustine's Law: Are We Really Headed for the $800 Billion-Dollar Fighter?* Lockheed Martin Aeronautics Company, Fort Worth, TX.

Kirkpatrick, D., and Pugh, P. (1983). Towards the Starship Enterprise – Are the Current Trends in Defence Unit Costs Inexorable? *Aerospace*, 10(5), 16–23.

Lee, P. (2019). An Ethics Framework for Autonomous Weapon Systems. *Air and Space Power Review*, 22(3), 60–81.

Markowski, S., Brauer, J., and Hartley, K. (2023). Augustine Investments and Weapons Systems. *Defence and Peace Economics*, 34(3), 293–307.

MoD (2022). *Evidence Summary: The Drivers of Cost Inflation*. Ministry of Defence, London, February.

NAO (2011). *Management of the Typhoon Project*. National Audit Office, London, HCP 755.

Nordlund, P. (2017). Defence-Specific Inflation – The Swedish Perspective, in Hartley, K., and Solomon, B. (eds.), *Defence Inflation* (ch. 6). Routledge, Abingdon. (Originally published in the April 2016 issue of *Defence and Peace Economics*, 27(2), 258–279.)

Overy, R. (2023). *Blood and Ruins: The Great Imperial War 1931–1945*. Penguin, London. (Originally published in 2021 by Allen Lane.)

Shah, R. M., and Kirchhoff, C. (2024). *Unit X*. Simon and Schuster, New York.

SIPRI (Stockholm International Peace Research Institute) (2024). SIPRI Arms Industry Database, December 2024, hwww.sipri.org/databases/armsindustry.

Sturmey, S. G. (1964). Cost Curves and Pricing in Aircraft Production. *Economic Journal*, LXXIV(296), 954–982.

Tisdell, C., and Hartley, K. (2008). *Microeconomic Policy: A New Perspective*. Edward Elgar, Cheltenham.

Weaver, H. (2022). Cost Escalation in Infrastructure Projects. *Ashurst*, 1 August, www.ashurst.com/en/insights/cost-escalation-in-infrastructure-projects/.

Welde, M., and Dahl, R. E. (2021). Cost Escalation in Road Construction Contracts. *Transportation Research Record*, 2675(9), 1006–1015.

Weston, P. J. (1996). Defence Research and Development: Encouraging Private Venture R&D with 'Option' Strategies. *Defence and Peace Economics*, 7(4), 313–324.

Wright, T. P. (1936). Factors Affecting the Cost of Airplanes. *Journal of the Aeronautical Sciences*, 3(4), 122–128.

Acknowledgements

The author is grateful for comments from Ben Solomon (Canada) and Derek Braddon (UK). The usual disclaimers apply.

Cambridge Elements

Defence Economics

Keith Hartley
University of York

Keith Hartley was Professor of Economics and Director of the Centre for Defence Economics at the University of York, where he is now Emeritus Professor of Economics. He is the author of over 500 publications comprising journal articles, books and reports. His most recent books include *The Economics of Arms* (Agenda Publishing, 2017) and with Jean Belin (Eds) *The Economics of the Global Defence Industry (*Taylor and Francis, 2020). Hartley was founding editor of the journal *Defence and Peace Economics*; a NATO Research Fellow; a QinetiQ Visiting Fellow; consultant to the UN, EC, EDA, UK MoD, HM Treasury, Trade and Industry, Business, Innovation and Skills and International Development and previously Special Adviser to the House of Commons Defence Committee.

About the Series

Defence Economics is a relatively new field within the discipline of economics. It studies all aspects of the economics of war and peace. It embraces a wide range of topics in both macroeconomics and microeconomics. *Cambridge Elements in Defence Economics* aims to publish original and authoritative papers in the field. These will include expert surveys of the foundations of the discipline, its historical development and contributions developing new and novel topics. They will be valuable contributions to both research and teaching in universities and colleges, and will also appeal to other specialist groups comprising politicians, military and industrial personnel as well as informed general readers.

Cambridge Elements

Defence Economics

Elements in the Series

Defence Economics: Achievements and Challenges
Keith Hartley

The Political Economy of Gulf Defense Establishments
Zoltan Barany

How Important are Superior Numbers?: A Reappraisal of Lanchester's Square Law
David L. I. Kirkpatrick

The Economics of Conflict and Peace: History and Applications
Shikha Basnet Silwal, Charles H. Anderton, Jurgen Brauer, Christopher J. Coyne and J. Paul Dunne

The US Defence Economy
Jomana Amara and Raymond E. Franck

Defence Acquisition and Procurement: How (Not) to Buy Weapons
Ron P. Smith

Britain and the Political Economy of European Military Aerospace Collaboration, 1960–2023
Keith Hayward

Defence Economics and Innovation
Gustavo Fornari Dall'Agnol

The Political Economy of Augustine Weapons
Keith Hartley

A full series listing is available at: www.cambridge.org/EDEC

For EU product safety concerns, contact us at Calle de José Abascal, 56–1º,
28003 Madrid, Spain or eugpsr@cambridge.org.

www.ingramcontent.com/pod-product-compliance
Lightning Source LLC
LaVergne TN
LVHW011856060526
838200LV00054B/4374